Avenues *to* *the* Heart

Teachers Who
Made a Difference

LARRY BLACKMER
EXECUTIVE EDITOR

Pacific Press® Publishing Association
Nampa, Idaho
Oshawa, Ontario, Canada
www.pacificpress.com

This book is dedicated to the thousands of Adventist teachers who have not only shared their professional expertise with their students through the years but shared themselves and the Lord they love and serve. Because of their dedicated service, the Seventh-day Adventist system of education is not only one of the best in the world, it is one that continues to provide educational and spiritual avenues to the heart.

Special thanks to Ann Fisher for editing the submitted stories, to Mark Haynal, Ed.D., for your support and commitment to the project, and to Walla Walla College for your support by providing the office space and personnel who solicited, collected, edited, and proofed the stories for publication. Finally, our thanks to all of those who submitted stories for this book, because without you this project would not be possible.

Larry Blackmer, executive editor
Layout and cover design by MCM Design Studio, mcmds.com
Typeset in Adobe Garamond and Univers Thin Ultra Condensed

Published by Pacific Press® Publishing Association
Printed in the United States of America

Additional copies of this book are available by phone, toll free 1-800-765-6955, or online at adventistbookcenter.com

---

ISBN 13: 978-0-8163-2173-5
ISBN 10: 0-8163-2173-6

Contents

Contents

Contents

Foreword

My family was introduced to Jesus in northern Wisconsin. There hadn't been much of a spiritual life in our home. But, the head elder gave us Bible studies, we became Seventh-day Adventist Christians, and I was enrolled in the Adventist elementary school.

In that school, in Merrill, Wisconsin, Mrs. Doyle taught me to pray. I'd never had that experience before. Mrs. Doyle taught our family about the Sabbath and how to keep it. She taught me, and I explained it to my parents. One day my mother said, "If Mrs. Doyle said it in church school, it must be right, so we have to do it." Mrs. Doyle had a lot of influence on the way we did things around our house.

Adventist teachers like Mrs. Doyle have made a positive difference in the homes and lives of our children for generations. To celebrate that life-changing influence, North American Division church members were asked to share their stories about Adventist teachers who had a special influence in their lives. This book is a compilation of their best stories.

Teachers have a hard row to hoe, and most don't choose the profession for its monetary rewards. Most teach because they love children and want to see them saved in God's kingdom. There are many teachers who have not heard a positive word from parents or constituents for a long time. When bad things happen around school, many of us feel compelled to speak to school staff about what is going wrong. But how often do we thank them for the good things that are happening?

As you read these stories about dedicated Adventist teachers and the difference they have made in the lives of their student storytellers, don't forget to look for the good things that are happening at your own Adventist school. Take every opportunity to hug a teacher and say Thank you!

Don C. Schneider, president
North American Division

Ralph

Niels Erik Andreasen

His name was Ralph, but I never dared call him that, for he was my science teacher, and I was but a sixteen-year-old student. I appreciated him because of his kindness, calm demeanor, and obvious brilliance. But most of us students were more attracted to another teacher—someone charismatic, flamboyant, and with exceptional public-speaking appeal. Ralph, on the other hand, was quiet and thoughtful. I am sure our student responses to these two different teacher personalities were influenced to a great degree by our impressionable, youthful minds. I recall speaking about these two teachers to my parents during school breaks, and I vaguely remember that they were cautious about my enthusiastic report of "the other" teacher.

"Have you gotten to know Ralph?" they inquired.

"Not really," I replied, "but I do like his classes."

Years passed, and though the memory of those early academy years has faded somewhat, one thing stands out clearly in my mind. Toward the end of the school year, I was running down the stairs in front of the administration building, on my way somewhere in a hurry, and Ralph was on his way up those same stairs in his calm dignity. He stopped me cold at the halfway point and asked to talk with me—something he had never done before in just that way. I immediately felt that something important was about to happen, but all he asked me was, "What are you going to do with your life?"

"I'm not sure," I replied with all the certainty of a sixteen-year-old. "My aunt wants me to study medicine, since I enjoy science, but I don't like to see blood."

"Well, how about becoming a teacher?" Ralph asked.

A teacher! I knew of only one person in our extended family who was a teacher, and I had never thought of that as a profession.

"And what would I teach?" I inquired in an effort to sound light-hearted, mature, and a bit of a smart aleck at the same time. But Ralph was serious.

"Science—you could teach science here," he replied.

"But you do that," I responded.

"Yes," he replied, "but not forever. We need another science teacher here, and that could be you. See to it," he urged and continued up the steps, leaving me standing there thinking about all the rest of my life with the limited tools of a sixteen-year-old.

That was the end of our conversation—only a few minutes, but they changed my life. To this day I do not know why I paid so much attention to this brief encounter, but I think it was because of Ralph, this calm, thoughtful, and brilliant man. Somehow I felt obligated to listen to him— perhaps the only teacher I have listened to with such careful attention.

Accordingly, the next day I called my parents, told them about this conversation, and asked them to make appointments for me to seek admission to the university matriculation course in math and natural science. It was a three-year program with difficult admission requirements, but I made it. Eventually, I studied at two universities and became a teacher myself.

Looking back on that life-changing conversation, after many years of working in education, I offer three simple conclusions. First, teachers have much more influence on the lives of their students than they imagine, even teachers who are not charismatic, so long as they are effective and thoughtful. Second, much of that influence does not happen in the classroom, but in conversations after or between classes—in the office, the hallways, or even on the stairs! Third, next to parents, teachers have the greatest impact on the future lives of their students and, therefore, on the future values and general direction of our society and community of faith.

Winston Churchill once described the efforts of—and the corresponding debt of obligation on the part of—the British public to the Royal Air Force (RAF) during World War II in this way: "Never . . . have so many owed so much to so few." That sentiment regarding the RAF could apply equally to all the "Ralphs" in the world.

Niels Erik Andreasen writes from Berrien Springs, Michigan, where he serves as Andrews University president.

A Life-Changing Difference

She was a smoking "flapper" with short skirts, short hair, and painted face—my new seventh-grade teacher. My school cronies and I were smokers, too. We fed our new taste by picking up cigarette butts. Taking the shortcut home through an orchard, I covered the stench of my filthy habit with apples. My godly, loving parents never found out.

But God knew and had a remedy. Mother's prayers for a Christian education for her children were providentially answered.

Abruptly, Dad's work changed. So in October 1925, we moved to South Lancaster, Massachusetts, where I was enrolled in the Atlantic Union College normal school's seventh grade. Miss Olive Lindberg was my new teacher. There was a glint in her eye and a captivating smile on her face. She played with us. She prayed with us. She read to us. We had parties together. She loved us!

The conference educational superintendent came to that sacred, happy schoolroom. He talked to us about living for Jesus and made an appeal. I stood to my feet. I made the decision of my life to be a worker for Jesus.

By God's grace, I have been privileged to spend forty-two years as a pastor. Now, at age ninety-three, I still thank God for Olive Lindberg and Adventist education, which made such a life-changing difference for me.

Benjamin F. Hartman writes from his home in the Smoky Mountains near Bryson City, North Carolina. He is a retired pastor who still works six to eight hours a day leading people to Jesus.

A Moment of Grace

When I was in the sixth grade (1969–1970), I was in Mrs. Eleanor
Nelson's class. During those years, the school had a strict policy about the
length of skirts the girls wore. If her skirt was too short, the girl was sent
home, along with a note describing the infraction. There had even been a
time when the girls were called into the school chapel and asked to kneel
down, while their skirts were measured to see if they met the guidelines.

In those days I lived in a single-parent, limited-income home. My
father lived in a different state, and I did not often see him. My mother
worked the night shift as a nurse and often didn't get home from her job
until after I had gone to school. My older sister and brother and I were
responsible for getting up in the morning and getting ourselves to school.

One day, as I was getting ready for school, my sister urged me
to wear a skirt she had recently worn. It was a mini skirt that was so
embarrassingly short, it hardly covered the bare essentials. Fortunately, I
was blissfully unaware of how short my skirt really was, because my older
sister had told me it looked great on me. "You look better in that skirt
than you have ever looked," she said. I was excited about my new look and
eager to show my school friends.

Needless to say, my skirt was far shorter than school policy allowed.
As I was sitting in class early that morning, the registrar came to the room
and asked me to go with her. I was still blissfully unaware of my situation.
She took me outside, and we got into her car. Instead of taking me home

to change my clothes and get in trouble with my mother, she took me shopping for new clothes. She bought me a new blouse, a skirt, and a jumper. As we shopped for the clothes, she taught me little tricks about shopping. After our shopping trip was over, she took me back to school in my brand-new clothes. I returned to class, still blissfully unaware of what had really happened.

In the years to come, I thought about that incident, and I came to realize that I was the recipient of a moment of grace. My life did not change much at that time—we were still poor, and my mother still had to work long hours away from home. But in later years, that incident became a beacon in my life that showed me an example of grace and redemption.

I don't remember the name of the registrar, and I no longer have any of the yearbooks from my grade-school days. We children merely called her "Registrar." I was told many years later that it was my teacher, Mrs. Nelson, who paid for my new clothes. I don't know if that is true, but I do know she was a wonderful teacher who believed in me. And I've never doubted she was involved in that gracious act of redemption.

Joy Graves writes from Lynnwood, Washington, where she works as a family therapist.

A Teacher to Imitate

PAUL KILGORE

Mr. Allan Hillier was principal and my ninth- and tenth-grade teacher at the junior academy in Rochester, New York, in 1949 and 1950. I don't remember the actual class work, but I remember what his life has meant to me.

Mr. Hillier loved music—male quartets in particular. There were only six boys in the ninth and tenth grades that year. When it was Ingathering time, Mr. Hillier told us that we were going to form a quartet and go downtown to sing for donations. Mr. Hillier was a baritone. We had a boy with a good bass voice for a fourteen-year-old. We also had a boy with a steady, strong voice to sing the lead. Mr. Hillier turned to me and said, "Paul, you will be the first tenor." What a surprise! Like most boys that age, I was trying to sing bass, and he was asking me—no, telling me—that I was to sing first tenor. That was the beginning of my love for male quartets.

Mr. Hillier was also a printer who had worked his way through college in a print shop. Someone gave our school a small letter press and two trays of type. He taught us beginning printing, a trade that I followed for most of my academy and college experience.

Mr. Hillier had a Model A Ford that was just large enough for our whole class to squeeze into. We had many wonderful field trips in that old car.

I have even more respect for Mr. Hillier now, when I realize that teachers at that time were paid for only nine months' work. He had to find other means during the summer to survive.

We students knew that Mr. Hillier loved the Lord—and all of us boys, too—with all his heart. He was soft-spoken and always smiling. What Mr. Hillier gave to me was a direction in life. What he *was* rubbed off on my life much more than what he *said*. I'm happy to be an imitator of his life.

Paul Kilgore, retired educator, boys' dean, principal, superintendent of schools, and director of education, writes from Cleveland, Tennessee.

Advice, Please

AIMEE LEUKERT

"How do I stop biting my fingernails?"

"How come boys are so mean?"

"Should I cut my hair?"

"Sarah and Jane aren't talking to me."

"I'm scared about moving."

"I told Susie a secret, and she's telling everyone!"

"I think Ron likes me. What should I do?"

"Do you think I'm fat?"

The questions poured out of my pen, fast and furious. Miss J. had us fill out a newspaper template each week as one of our English assignments. We could headline it however we chose and write the articles we wished—book reviews, current events, interviews, sports recaps, etc. Writing quality came first, content second. In my newspapers, I always included an advice column.

Ten is a difficult age for girls—at least I remember thinking so. I remember feeling not yet cool enough to hang out with the junior-high students, but too old for the little kids. I remember unstable emotions, unpredictable mood swings, and an insecure self-image. I remember awkward confrontations with boys, overdramatic fights with girls, and struggles with conformity and peer pressure. But in the midst of all the turmoil of this pre-adolescent stage, I remember Miss J.'s calm, quiet voice speaking to me through her replies.

No matter how silly the question or how small the concern, she always replied. In her neat, all-capital-letters script, she wrote back—sometimes a phrase or two, sometimes a whole page. Gently, never scolding, never patronizing, Miss J.'s responses always prodded me to look at the big picture, to think about the other person first, to react and respond in a Christlike manner. She challenged me to be the bigger person. She applauded when I succeeded and consoled when I failed.

I marvel now at the time she must have set aside to respond to these "advice columns"—time that could have been spent writing lesson plans or grading papers. Time that could have been spent answering phone calls or creating new projects. Time that could have been spent tidying up her desk or working on the upcoming school fair. But Miss J. took time for me. And because of her, I take time for my students.

I, too, am a fifth-grade teacher now. And I, too, have students who turn in journals for me to read and respond to. And though there are many days when my desk is piled high with papers, my to-do list beckons, and the temptation rises to just place a check in the grade book, I don't. Instead, I sit. And I read. I read about my students' concerns and worries and questions. I read about the latest class gossip, about pets that died, about parents who are divorcing. And then I reply. Sometimes a phrase or two, sometimes a whole page.

I do this because I remember what it was like to be ten years old and how, through *my* teacher's replies, I felt special and loved and cherished.

Aimee (Saesim) Leukert writes from Simi Valley, California, where she is a fifth-grade teacher at Crescenta Valley Adventist School. Aimee is still in contact with her former teacher, Mrs. Jackee Clodio.

Anywhere With Jesus I Can Safely Go

GRETCHEN PIKE

Laughter and shouts filled the air as students rushed out for recess. But Wava Anderson's eyes were riveted on me, a ninth-grader whose face was white as a sheet. I walked slowly, eyes straight ahead, as if in terrible shock. Mrs. Anderson thought, "Oh, what can I do to help that sad girl?" Once again, fellow students were teasing and ridiculing me.

The year was 1956. The place was Minneapolis Seventh-day Adventist Junior Academy. The teacher, Wava (Holm) Anderson. Several years earlier, about a year after her marriage in 1945 to Eric Anderson, the Minnesota Conference president had explained to Mrs. Anderson that although there were no funds available, the Minneapolis Junior Academy needed a music teacher. She accepted the challenge and threw all of her energies into building a first-class music department.

Mrs. Anderson was not only an extremely skilled music teacher, but she also had a unique gift, put there by God, to reach out with love and compassion to all her students and make them feel special, no matter what their problems might be. I felt drawn to Mrs. Anderson's compassion and caring ways, and over time I began to confide in her about my troubled life.

I had been born with a rare birth defect in an era when such misfortunes were not openly talked about. I think my mother was ashamed of me, and she didn't want anyone to know about my physical problems. I was home-schooled for my first six years of school. When I was finally sent to a "regular" Adventist church school in the seventh grade, I was right up with the other kids scholastically, but I didn't know the first thing about how to get along socially. In addition, my parents were constantly fighting at home. I scarcely knew what love was. Neither I nor my parents received any counseling. Mrs. Anderson was the only person I could confide in, the first solid ray of light in my life.

As that ninth-grade school year progressed, I learned far more than how to improve my piano technique. I also learned that there was at least *one* person who really cared and who was willing to listen to a young, physically handicapped girl who desperately needed love and understanding. Mrs. Anderson profoundly affected my life.

In spite of the fact that our lives touched for only one short year, a lifelong friendship resulted between us. Mrs. Anderson and I kept in touch until her death in 1994. She once told me, during one of our long-distance phone conversations, that I was one of ten people she wanted to play the piano with in heaven. During another long-distance conversation we had a few months before Mrs. Anderson died, she sang *a cappella* to me over the phone, "Anywhere With Jesus I Can Safely Go." I will cherish that very meaningful memory of Mrs. Anderson until the end of my life.

Gretchen (Rohlf) Pike writes from Beatrice,
Nebraska, where she is retired with
her husband, Dannie.

As Long as I Am Able

WINONA HUDSON

"In all thy ways acknowledge him, and he shall direct thy paths" (Proverbs 3:6) is the text that comes to my mind when I think of one of my most inspirational teachers. She was born in Chicago and wanted to be an archeologist, but her mother would not allow it. So she became a teacher. She often told us stories of being chased after school by students because she didn't fit in as a light-skinned, long-haired African American.

Mrs. Verlean Knight had four children. She made a vow to the Lord that if He would allow her to put her children in an Adventist Christian school, she would be in His service as a missionary teacher. She and the Lord were solely responsible for her childrens' Christian education. She did not make much money during the 1960s, since women were not considered the head of the household and could not receive the same pay allotment as men. Because her husband's work was seasonal, keeping her children in school seemed impossible. But with God all things are possible if you believe, and Verlean Knight believed. People often tried to persuade her to go into public school teaching so that she could make more money. But she always said, "I made a promise to the Lord that if He would allow me to keep my children in a Christian school, I would serve Him as long as I live." So we stopped pressuring her to leave church school. Instead we watched as God used her and spared her life as she worked for Him.

One October, while she was on yard duty, she had an allergy attack. After one of her sneezing spells, a stream of blood rushed from her nose.

She did all she could to stop the bleeding, but it poured out as if a water hose had burst. Staff members ran to her, held her by each arm, and tried to stop the bleeding. When the ambulance arrived, she went into cardiac arrest due to blood loss. All she could hear was the voices of the paramedics trying to make decisions as they continued CPR to the nearest hospital.

"There is no use; she's not going to make it," one voice said. Then she heard another voice say, "No, we are not giving up; we are not going to let her die." In her mind she was thinking, "I can't die, my kids need me." I thought she was talking about us, her children, but, no, she was talking about the kids at school. "They are going to get behind. Who is going to teach them their sounds and how to read? I can't die." After a year of four brain surgeries and thirteen angiograms, she returned to Los Angeles Adventist Academy to continue teaching first grade.

Mrs. Knight is my mother, and her dedication and inspiration have inspired me to always acknowledge God so that He will direct my paths. Her determination to do the Lord's will has allowed me to become the person that I am and will continue to become.

Today, after she has spent thirty-eight years of service in the Adventist school system, you will find Mrs. Knight in the first-grade classroom at Los Angeles Adventist Academy. And if you ask her why she is still there, she will say, "As long as I am able, I will let God use me to do His service."

Winona Hudson writes from Fresno, California. She has served as a registered nurse, an elementary teacher, and a school administrator.

"Aunt Nancy"

CATHERINE LAMBERT

I was a new immigrant, freshly arrived on the British Columbia coast from Yorkshire, England. I was twelve years old and apprehensive about starting in a new school. In England, the cane and the ruler were the disciplinary methods used to encourage scholastic achievement. What would Canadian education and my new teacher be like?

We lived on a floating logging camp—a dozen houses built on huge log floats with three hundred feet of water beneath. On the first day of classes, I entered my new, one-room school with some anxiety; children had already teased me about my British accent. The teacher, Mrs. Nancy Gildersleeve, welcomed me, introduced me to the class, and assigned me a desk behind her daughter, Heather. The school day began with hymn singing and a devotional, after which Mrs. Gildersleeve began to pray for each student by name.

Soon I was immersed in long division and subordinate clauses. Mrs. Gildersleeve, whom we affectionately called "Aunt Nancy," became my angel of liberation from ignorance. At the end of my eighth-grade year, she planned a graduation ceremony for my twin brother and me—her only eighth-grade students that year—and for the ninth-grade students. I remember sitting in my bedroom after the ceremony, in my long, silk dress, not wanting the wonderful experience to end. I determined to become a teacher like "Aunt Nancy," and I still cherish *The Church Hymnal* and Bible that were presented to me as graduation gifts that day.

Over the course of fifty years, "Aunt Nancy" kept in touch with me. She always believed in me, always encouraged me, and prayed for me. The firm, but kind, discipline she administered in her classroom and the thorough grounding she gave me in English grammar and math stood me in good stead throughout my high school and college days. I also learned my first Adventist hymns in her classroom and learned to love Jesus best of all!

Today, as I stand in front of my students in my one-room school in a northern Canadian community, her influence still lives on. I pray that I may pass on to my students the positive impact that "Aunt Nancy" left on my life and character. I look forward to meeting her in heaven to tell her how thankful I have been for her example. "Aunt Nancy" was my first Canadian teacher. She was the best!

Catherine Lambert writes from Terrace, British Columbia, Canada, where she is a teaching principal at Spring Creek Adventist School.

Blessed Are the Peacemakers

EMILY THOMSEN

"I like your shirt," I told my friend Rachel on a Sabbath afternoon hike not long ago.

"Oh, thanks," Rachel smiled as she looked down at the shirt. Then she added proudly, "I got it at Old Navy for only ten bucks!"

"Emily, you're always giving compliments!" Haley chimed in. "I like that about you!"

Feeling modest, I thanked Haley and then explained how I had acquired the habit.

As a third-grader at Foothills Adventist Elementary School in Deer Park, California, I found myself in the middle of a group of girls who could not seem to get along. I would like to blame the problem on two particularly cliquish little girls, but I am sure that, in reality, we were all to blame to some degree. Calling each other names, accusing each other of stealing, ridiculing each other for things we could not change, being exclusive and hurting each other's feelings—these were just some of our little crimes. Children can be so hard on each other!

Tall Miss Linda Maynard, with her black curly hair, olive skin, and dark twinkling eyes, had already been established in my mind as a favorite teacher. She must have had a difficult time that year, teaching both third and fifth grades in the same classroom, with a passel of disgruntled little girls to boot! Nevertheless, she managed to make the classroom a fun place and developed an inventive technique to pacify our girlish quarrels and foster friendships among us.

One day during recess, Miss Maynard gathered all of us third-grade girls together and handed us each a notebook. We were to write the names of all our girl classmates in our notebooks, one on each page. Our assignment, to last the rest of the school year, was to give one compliment each week to every girl in the class and record the compliments in our notebooks.

I undertook this task with enthusiasm. My little pink notebook filled with entries such as, "October 15, Cerise Senter: 'I like your watch.' " Or, "November 10, Amy Bauer: 'I like your shirt.' " Or, "March 3, Isabel Rubalcalva: 'I like your shoes.' " Gradually the tension between us girls eased, and we were able to play together without difficulty.

Come to think of it, I do not remember any of the compliments I received. But I still remember how important it is to let people know they are appreciated. It was Miss Maynard's inventiveness that cultivated in me the habit of complimenting other people when they wore something I liked, did something I appreciated, or had some characteristic I admired.

Thank you, Miss Maynard. You were a great teacher!

Emily Thomsen writes from Collegedale, Tennessee, where she works as a wellness professional and massage therapist.

Blue Jeans and a Stolen Kiss

STACEY TOL

They were not the easiest teachers at Milo Adventist Academy in Days Creek, Oregon. In fact, if you were to ask any student on campus who the hardest teacher was, odds were it would be Alfred or Cheryl Andrieux.

He taught advanced placement history, physics, economics, and many other study-your-brains-out-to-pass classes. She taught English. Her job was not to teach Shakespeare or Dickens, rather the science of English— structure, grammar, and spelling.

His favorite color was gray; her favorite was green. They dressed accordingly. Mrs. Andrieux's room was the only one in the entire administration building that was not white. It was light green. At the beginning of our junior year, she told us veteran students, with a smirk, that someone had mistakenly painted her room white that summer. We laughed at such a rookie mistake. Of course, by then the room had been repainted in its original green.

Mr. and Mrs. Andrieux could be intimidating. Woe to the student caught sleeping in Mr. Andrieux's class! You could consider yourself lucky if he chose to wake you by dropping a four-inch-thick history book on the floor beside your desk.

Mrs. Andrieux was the great detector of blue jeans and chewing gum— both strictly forbidden. It became a challenge for students to sneak one or the other past her for an entire period. Many tried. Many failed.

Despite their deadpan demeanors, they were both compassionate. Once, I recall, I had a new wool sweater with nothing to match it but blue jeans. Although my seat at the time was near the back of the class, Mrs. Andrieux still detected them. As a "village" student, I couldn't go back to the dorm to change, but was given a warning not to wear them again. Later that day, I met her in the hallway. "I didn't notice before," she said, "but that's a very pretty sweater."

Another time, my boyfriend (now my husband) and I were stealing a kiss in a corner, when who should appear in our peripheral vision? Mr. Andrieux! Our indiscretion could have put us on "social," a separation penalty for couples. We quickly turned and walked nonchalantly away, trying to pretend nothing had happened. Mr. Andrieux also walked in our direction and, mercifully, also pretended nothing had happened.

Whether they purposefully cultivated their mystique or not, I don't know. Regardless, Mr. and Mrs. Andrieux were both wonderful teachers. They had a solid grasp of their subjects and earnestly sought to convey their knowledge to a bunch of hormone-distracted teenagers. They succeeded. Go ahead—ask me about prepositional phrases or supply-and-demand economics.

Post-academy and sometimes post-college, a lot of career decisions have to be made. Choosing from the innumerable possibilities is not easy. That's why it is so significant to me that two people with so much talent decided it was best spent in teaching. Multitudes of students, before and after my time, have sat before them, come to love them, and most importantly, have really learned from them.

Communicating the dedication and knowledge of two such competent teachers is not easy. I hope I have succeeded, but mostly, I hope I haven't misspelled anything.

Stacey (Harman) Tol writes from Ormond Beach, Florida. Married to her academy sweetheart, she's an at-home mom with three young children.

Creative Learning at Its Best

KELLY MARIE JAMES

"Beep! Beeeeep!"

"Kelly?"

"Harry Truman."

"That's correct. Five points for Mr. Blah team."

The handmade mascot representing Mr. Blah, my team, was pushed a few inches on its string across the ceiling, taking the lead. Mr. Bursey continued with the next question.

"Who was the founder of the Settlement House Movement and the NAACP?"

"Beep! Beep!" The classroom exploded with the sound of fifth- to eighth-grade students "beeping" frantically.

"Sam?"

"Jane Addams."

"Right. Spell Czechoslovakia backwards for extra points."

And so went a typical morning in Ken Bursey's classroom at Camelback Thunderbird Elementary in Scottsdale, Arizona, now renamed Thunderbird Christian Elementary.

When one looked into Mr. Bursey's fifth- through eighth-grade classroom, it was evident that his classes were anything but typical. Simply entering the room required careful navigation of bookcases, computer tables, desks arranged in groups of four, and couches. A giant parachute draped down from the ceiling, diffusing harsh fluorescent light, and the walls were decorated with posters and pictures of famous people and places.

This was the classroom in which I first read Plato, Socrates, and *Animal Farm* by George Orwell. I stood in front of Mr. Bursey's desk dressed as Harry Truman and Grace Kelly (not at the same time), reciting speeches to the class in first person. History came alive in the form of the song, "We Didn't Start the Fire," by Billy Joel, as our class learned the significance of each word and phrase. Names of famous historical people were connected to faces as we were tested on their pictures hanging on the walls.

Years later, portions of my high school senior history and advanced-placement English classes were simply reviews of what Mr. Bursey taught me from fifth through eighth grades. That knowledge remained vividly in my mind, thanks to such creative teaching strategies as re-enacting World War I on the playground, with sponges instead of rifles, taking one step toward or away from the enemy with each blast from Mr. Bursey's trumpet. I remember spending hours carving out life-sized bones from thick sponge board and creating human organs from balloons. For weeks we ducked around the classroom to avoid the three-dimensional skeletons hanging from the ceiling.

Science projects included building towers or bridges with toothpicks. After weeks of careful architectural planning, our creations were tested on the basketball court. Weight after weight was added until the structure splintered and crashed, or simply bent over sideways like taffy from the excessive glue used by its creator.

Not all learning in Mr. Bursey's classroom was hands-on. I memorized more vocabulary words in his classes than I did for my SAT or GRE. We also spent an entire year learning the names of countries, their capitals, and their three major exports. By the end of the year, we were required to fill in a completely blank map of the world with everything we had learned.

To further our knowledge of the world, we picked a country as "our" country. Over the course of the year, we wrote reports on "our" country, presented them to the class, and basically became experts on that country. I have a fondness for Luxembourg to this day because of that assignment.

I could go on and on with examples of Mr. Bursey's creativity and genius. He exposed me to a world of learning I never dreamed could exist. I came away from his class with a love of learning and an appreciation for questioning authority (our class motto by the way). And in case you were wondering, nearly all of us could spell Czechoslovakia backwards by the end of the year.

Kelly Marie James writes from Orem, Utah, where she is pursuing a Ph.D. in clinical neuro-psychology at Brigham Young University.

Dr. Millie

Kathy-ann Hernandez

The day I arrived on the campus of Andrews University in Berrien Springs, Michigan, as a graduate student from Trinidad, things did not go as planned. The promised graduate assistantship that would help finance my education was no longer available. What was I going to do? Anxiously, I searched the bulletin board in the School of Education for job openings. "Please God, let there be something I can do," I prayed. Then I saw it:

Wanted: Graduate Assistant
Position: To work as administrative assistant for
Family Life International (FLI)

I called my advisor and asked him to recommend me and set up an appointment. "Lord, help me to get this job. You know I need it," I whispered as I walked into the FLI office for the interview. That's when I met her—Dr. Millicent Youngberg.

Even though it was early January and several degrees below zero, I was sweating underneath my newly acquired wool sweater. I felt uncomfortable and uncertain. What would it be like interacting professionally with a Caucasian? Would she like me? Would my accent be a deterrent? Fears! Fears! Fears!

Dr. Youngberg immediately put me at ease with her gentle manner. She reviewed my resume, asked intelligent questions, and spoke to me as though

2—A. T. T. H.

33

I had already been given the job. "Kathy-ann, your job will include meeting with clients, answering questions, and providing information," she said, smiling. "You can call me Dr. Millie. When can you start?" My jaw dropped.

My first day on the job brought pleasant surprises. Before I could take my seat, Dr. Millie suggested that we begin with prayer. Next she was handing me forms to fill out so I could have my own office keys. She even gave me the passwords to the telephone, fax machine, and copier. "Is this woman crazy?" I thought. "She hardly knows me, yet she trusts me with so much." This trust became the foundation of our relationship.

I worked with Dr. Millie for the entire length of my stay at Andrews University. Even when a vacancy became available for a position with my advisor, I did not want to leave, and she did not want me to leave either. We were a team!

During that time, I was impressed with her commitment to the FLI ministry. Director of Family Life International was not just her job title; it was an outgrowth of her personal ministry. It was obvious from the start that she cared about me not only as an employee; she cared about me as a person. "Kathy-ann," she said, "if your school work gets too difficult and you need time off to study, let me know." She told me I was free to use the computers to type my papers, and if I needed materials for presentations, all I needed to do was ask. One morning as she walked into the office, I glimpsed a hint of bright yellow. "Surprise," she said, "these are for you—daffodils, the first flowers of spring."

I left Andrews in 1997, prematurely, to take a teaching position in the British Virgin Islands. When I returned the following summer to complete my degree, I went to Dr. Millie's office for a quick visit. She was very busy, but stopped and greeted me with an exuberant hug. After some quick catching up, I confided in her, "Dr. Millie, I am so nervous about my comprehensive exam." She immediately walked to the door and closed it. "Come, let's pray about it," she said.

The day of the exam I sat waiting anxiously in Bell Hall with the other students. My head was bent, when I felt a hand on my shoulder. I looked up. It was Dr. Millie's husband, Dr. John Youngberg. "Let's walk up the steps," he said. I followed him. "Kathy-ann, my wife commissioned me to find you and pray with you this morning." As we bowed our heads in prayer, my heart was full, and there were tears in my eyes—she had remembered me!

Graduation day was bittersweet. None of my relatives could make the expensive trip. When I walked up to receive that hard-earned diploma, I heard shouts of "Yeah, Kathy-ann." I looked in the direction of the shouts and saw the excited faces of my colleagues from the FLI office. I did not see Dr. Millie, but I was certain she was there. After the ceremony, I was busy taking pictures. In the midst of my exhilaration, I heard a familiar voice calling my name; it was Dr. Millie. "Kathy-ann," she said, "I am so proud of you." She reached over and hugged me, then she handed me a bouquet of flowers and a sealed envelope.

Dr. Millie is not one to publish her good works, and I know that she will be a bit embarrassed by this. Don't be, Dr. Millie. My life has been greatly enriched by touching yours.

*Kathy-ann C. Hernandez, Ph.D., is an assistant professor
of educational psychology and assessment at Eastern
University in St. Davids, Pennsylvania.*

Encouragement for My Childhood Dreams

JOHN MARTIN

In the sixth grade I attended church school in Carthage, Illinois. There were only four students in the school that year, and at the end of the year the church made the painful decision to close the school. The teacher was Jean Taylor. I think it was her first year of teaching. I don't remember a lot about the schoolwork we did. It must have been satisfactory, because I went on to be very successful in academia. What I do remember is Miss Taylor encouraging me with my "impossible childhood dreams."

With only four students, she had more flexibility than a teacher would have had in a larger school. When we took field trips, she simply put the whole school in her car, and off we went, often with very little advance planning. Those field trips were wonderful. We learned how cardboard boxes are made, how potato chips are made, and many other marvelous things to a sixth-grader.

That year I had a fixation on shuffleboard. I was from a financially struggling family, and to buy a shuffleboard set was out of the question. So I decided I wanted to make a set. Miss Taylor encouraged me in my dream. Out of her limited school funds, she bought a tiny power jigsaw, and when I had finished my schoolwork, I was allowed to go to the furnace room and work on my "project." I had only the crudest of materials—some old, yellow pine boards someone had left in the furnace room years before. But under Miss

Taylor's encouragement, I did make a very nice shuffleboard set that year.

Once the year was over, I don't remember ever using my shuffleboard, but the lessons I learned about being patient and following my dreams have stayed with me all my life.

John Martin is a retired pastor who writes from LaSalle, Colorado.

From Anger to Love

During my junior year at Great Lakes Academy, the administration decided that, even though we already had three deans, the school would add a fourth task force dean. This made me angry! We had enough people watching us and telling us what to do. We were good, responsible girls. Why did we need one more dean?

So when the new dean came in January, I was not friendly at all. She had the early morning shift and was there to greet us as we went to breakfast or class. She always had a happy smile on her face as she greeted us with a friendly "Good morning" or "Hello." I found this annoying. It also annoyed me that girls would gather in her office when she was on duty to chat or just hang out. I would walk by and glare.

Then one Friday afternoon in late January, something drew me into her office. I only sat and listened as the other girls talked. But as the conversation developed, the dean began asking me questions to draw me in. We discovered that our birthdays were only one day apart (plus or minus a few years!) and that we would celebrate them the very next week. That was our bonding moment.

She and I became peas in a pod. We always hung out together when she was in the dorm. And even when she was off duty, we did fun things together. One event that I particularly remember was going on a Mother's Day canoe trip without a canoe. We floated down the river. We spent so much time together that people would ask me where she was and ask her where I was.

From that bonding day in her office until she left Great Lakes Academy, she gave me a Bible promise card and a hug each day on my way out the door. I loved this, and something started changing in my heart.

There were times I could not study in all the noise, so I asked to study in her room. She always agreed and said that if she weren't there to just knock and go in. Every time I went to her room, I felt a peaceful presence. It was strange. When I told her about it, she said she had prayed for the Spirit of the Lord to dwell there. I guess He did.

These experiences led me to ask her more about her relationship with Jesus. She shared a lot from that point on, and so did I. We talked about personal stuff, relational stuff, and about God. She taught me how to start having my own personal relationship with Jesus. She got me into reading the Bible every day. She changed me from a person who grew up as an Adventist knowing about Jesus to a person who knows Jesus as her best Friend.

Thank you, Cyndi Tan.

Becky Gomoll writes from Clovis, California, were she works as a substitute teacher in the public school system.

From Socialite to Scholar

PENNY MOORE

As I entered the ninth grade at Elmshaven Church School in Tulsa, Oklahoma, too many years ago to tell, education was not a serious matter to me. Actually, it was a big social event. That's when I ran headlong into Dr. Daryl Beyer. While there was no physical collision, the experience was one that would change my life.

Dr. Beyer was strict and expected great things from his students. He believed in the Pygmalion effect, and each of his students blossomed under his care. For some reason, I did not want to disappoint him. It was not that I was afraid of him; it was just a deep respect and a desire to please.

Something had to change if I were to meet his expectations. I began to study from the time I got home from school until my mother insisted that the lights go out. The change that year has served me well for the rest of my life. I learned how to study and enjoy it.

Dr. Beyer had a way of making you believe all things were possible. He even made me believe that I could sing, although anyone who knows me can tell you he wasn't able to actually make it be true! Once he told me I did not read enough and that he doubted that I could read a real book. I think we had a kind of duel going on—"You say I cannot, so just watch me." I read *Mein Kampf.* I doubt that book was what Dr. Beyer had in mind, but it looked like a real, serious adult book to me.

Dr. Beyer had a way of showing that he cared without lowering the academic standard. If you earned an A in Dr. Beyer's class, you knew two things: You did earn it, and it did mean "outstanding." Nothing was rubber-stamped or given away. If you made a bad grade, it was all right to be sad or a bit discouraged, but Dr. Beyer would help you remember that in the educational process, earning grades is the student's responsibility.

Thank you, Dr. Beyer, for helping me learn how to study and for instilling a love for learning in my life. I think of you often and try to model some of your ways with my own students.

Penny (Wolfe) Moore, Ph.D., writes from Cleburne, Texas. She is a professor and chair of the nursing department at Southwestern Adventist University.

Great Balls of Fire

JUDY SHULTZ

The teacher who most affected my life was Joe Engelkemier, who was my Bible teacher for at least part of my junior high years at what was then known as Glendale Union Academy. His nickname, dubbed by some of his students, was "Holy Joe." The name was used derisively by some, but out of awe and respect by others.

I remember several evening activities at the Engelkemier home, where we had a lot of good times. However, even in a fun, social setting, the dedication and love the members of that home had for God was always evident.

The year I particularly remember was the year we studied *The Great Controversy*, focusing on end-time events. During one of our classes, Mr. Engelkemier was talking about the events that were to come. I can't be positive that this was the exact quote he used, but it was something like these words of Ellen G. White's found in *Evangelism*, page 29: "Great balls of fire were falling upon houses, and from these balls fiery arrows were flying in every direction. It was impossible to check the fires that were kindled, and many places were being destroyed." Unfortunately for Mr. Engelkemier, "Great Balls of Fire" also happened to be the title of a recently released rock and roll hit song performed by Jerry Lee Lewis. Even Jerry Lee Lewis called his music "the devil's music," and I'm absolutely positive that Mr. Engelkemier was totally unacquainted with Jerry Lee Lewis or his new hit song, but almost the entire class totally split up when he referred to "great balls of fire." Mr. Engelkemier was very gracious with us, but returned us to the topic at hand without too much delay.

I also remember what we thought was a horrendously long outline to memorize for a test. We were told that our test would simply be to reproduce that outline, which I believe I still have stored in a box of special things that I have kept over the years. The test came and went, but as the years progressed, the memory of that outline has not been completely erased. I still remember a lot of those upcoming events and the reassurances that were included, not only in the outline, but in Mr. Engelkemier's daily teaching. I knew he wanted each one of us not only to be ready for the trials that lay ahead but also to know how to trust in the calm assurance of God's love for us as individuals. He did not want us to have head knowledge of these events without heart knowledge and a genuine experience with Jesus as our personal Friend and Savior.

One of my classmate's siblings once stated how neat it would be, during the time of trouble, to be in the same remnant group in the mountains with Mr. Engelkemier. To me, that was a very high compliment of respect for him and his relationship with God as a personal friend. I still agree that it would be a very positive experience to be in that remnant group with Mr. Engelkemier, and I have absolutely no doubt in my mind that I will meet him in heaven even if our paths do not again cross on this earth.

*Judy Shultz is a registered nurse
who writes from Mill Spring,
North Carolina.*

My Favorite Teacher

SHIRLEY GREAR

My favorite teacher was tall and slender with a warm, compassionate smile. She had an expressive face that urged even the most inattentive students to realize when self-correction was their wisest choice. Her large brown eyes made frequent contact that seemed to pierce any soul, making excuses worthless. With a look, she could quiet a classroom or make us convulse with laughter. She was always there, never sick, and genuinely seemed to like us teenagers.

When my stepfather died, it was my favorite teacher who cared enough to let me cry on her shoulder, who drove me twenty miles home, and who frequently checked on my well-being. She would not tolerate petty injustices or prejudices and absolutely required that we treat everyone just as we would want to be treated. She was the underdog's crusader and the bully's Achilles' heel.

To me, as a young student, these were the qualities that made Phyllis Bryan Paytee, my Lynwood Academy English teacher, my favorite. Now as an adult, I have an expanded appreciation for her. She always represented the very best, always required the very best, and always made excellence seem attainable. At times, we students tried to rush through our assignments as quickly as possible. Mrs. Paytee, however, expected us to do our very best work, and assignments were never considered accomplished until they were finished correctly.

Mrs. Paytee was more than an English language instructor. She was an educator of life principles; a mentor, friend, and confidant; a consummate professional, and more. It seemed that she could draw endless lessons from any literary work. Some of the classical literature we studied made no sense until Mrs. Paytee read aloud to us and uncovered the relationship between timeless literature and our own lives.

We knew Mrs. Paytee was a Christian, not because she told us, but because of the way she handled the occasional tantrums, pranks, defiance, and mischief attempted by some. She knew how to make students feel that harmful misconduct truly did not become us, and that we were indeed too responsible to betray ourselves that way.

It is because of Mrs. Paytee that I now enjoy life as a freelance writer and motivational speaker. Presently, my favorite teacher serves as associate superintendent of schools in the Southern California Conference where she continues to help scores of teachers make learning a fascinating, lifelong adventure!

Shirley Grear writes from Abington, Pennsylvania, where she works as a bank systems analyst.

Wrestling With Christianity

When my brother, Bob, and I descended on Laurelwood Academy in late 1958, we presented the school with a challenge of no ordinary character. For openers, we were so diminutive the school registrar was forced to use a magnifying glass in order to register us for the school year! For the record, I was the second-to-the-shortest student in the school. Sigh! All the girls were as tall or taller than I was. I was sixteen years old, literally a human bonsai.

More challenging yet was the fact that we were not Seventh-day Adventists. Serious Christianity was still pretty much a novelty to us. Here we were, two outsiders entering into a rather bold Adventist educational experiment that featured the honor system, rigorous work (three to four hours a day at forty cents per hour), and a bunch of conservative, eagle-eyed educators with names like Gammon, Fullerton, Johnson, Ward, Burton, Canty, and Kaiser.

Forty-five years later, I'm still baffled by how we thrived while many of the children of the "saints" seemed only to talk about "getting out of this hole so we can have Cokes and hamburgers." Granted, the program was regimented and strict, yet my brother Bob noted with a touch of nostalgia while reminiscing recently, that the school somehow allowed him to roam the hills almost at will. The effort to maintain conformity and uniformity was adapted to meet the needs of his free spirit.

We had every right to get discouraged. Surely they spoke English in Bible classes, but for us it was as difficult as a foreign language. Hey, I didn't have the fuzziest idea who Moses was, and "Jesus" was a common curse word that we heard my father's workers use daily.

Until almost the end, we were unaware that our Bible teacher, Elder Benny Evans, was dying with cancer. On that fateful and final Friday evening as he stood in front of us, he looked like he was in the prime of life. As he talked to us about life and death, though, I noted a tiredness and sadness in his voice, and yet we students were electrified by some unknown presence. He told his story and then left us with a Bible text I have never forgotten. Bob and I had lost our mother to cancer a few years earlier. Maybe he was speaking more to his family than to us, but the text, "My God shall supply all your needs according to his riches in glory" (Philippians 4:19) was indelibly etched on my mind.

Weeks of prayer were special times. Bob and I gave our hearts to Jesus during one of them. Subsequently, we recommitted ourselves to Jesus time and time again. Friday nights always had those huge long lines where everyone "testified." I was scared spitless, but it was the "in" thing to do, so I did it.

One day, while I was struggling whether to become a Seventh-day Adventist Christian, I came upon two teachers, Mr. James Canty (history and government) and Mr. Vernon Kaiser (math), strolling toward the girls' dorm. It was an awesome spring day as they walked along in animated conversation, dressed in stiff white shirts and ties, every bit the grave educators they were. Then, like lightning, it happened. And what I saw changed my life.

I was too far away to hear exactly what they were talking about, but it was clear from their body language that their conversation was picking up in intensity. One of them grabbed the other and started tickling. Their laughing, tickling, and wrestling quickly escalated, until my reserved, sober teachers were in "full embrace" wrestling, first standing, then sprawled out on the lawn. I strained to watch the blur of flailing arms and legs as they wrestled, rolled, and laughed down the long, steep grassy hill in front of the girls' dorm.

I said to myself, "Wow! It must be fun to be a Christian. Hey, God! Count me in. I want to have as much fun as they are having." That was forty-five years ago. I'm still a Seventh-day Adventist Christian and following their example. I have a pile of fun every day.

John W. Ash III writes from Taiwan, Republic of China, where he serves as the president of the Taiwan Conference of Seventh-day Adventists. FYI, the "human bonsai" is now six-foot-two!

A Thirty-Day Dare

CAREL MOUNTAIN

By the time I was fourteen and a freshman in high school, I had decided that any form of God or religion wasn't for me. I had chosen friends who reflected those values, and during freshman Bible class we made it clear to our teacher, Mr. Kenneth Wilson, just how "uncool" it was to be a Christian.

Mr. Wilson was thirty, unmarried, and new to our school. Outspoken and direct, he came to Orangewood Academy in southern California from somewhere in Nebraska. He taught Bible and speech class, treating the students as if we were important and our opinions mattered. Although many of us liked the fact that he spoke to us on our level, it made us uncomfortable to imagine that which we could not fathom. Mr. Wilson's idea of heaven as whatever we loved here on earth, only better, was a new concept to us. "Do you love to snow ski?" he'd query. "What if there was a world just for snow skiing, where all the slopes went down and you never had to ride the lift? Wouldn't that be heaven?"

With remarks like these, he'd make us laugh, but he'd also make us think. He understood that our lives here were all we knew, and he related biblical ideas to our everyday world. By understanding the importance of our familiar world, he broke through the barrier of our concept of God as removed and distant, painting a picture of a God who was interested in us, even if we were only fourteen.

Freshman Bible class was the last period of the day. Impatient for school to be out, my friends and I would sit in the back of the classroom, talking, joking, and rolling our eyes. Despite our disrespectful attitudes, we were all honor students and would often pose uncomfortable questions just to see the class squirm. After a particularly controversial class period, Mr. Wilson asked four of us to stay after class. He said he understood our position, but he wanted us to participate in an experiment with him. "I dare each one of you to read your Bible for thirty days," he challenged. "At the end of that time, we'll get back together and you can tell me what you think. If you still haven't experienced the power of Jesus, then I'll leave you alone in Bible class."

Eager to prove that God was not powerful, we all accepted the challenge. By introducing us to the God he knew so well—the loving God, the father God, a God whose world included teenagers—Mr. Wilson had sparked an interest in us. His enlightening ideas about the love of Jesus and the challenge of an experiment reached four teenagers who otherwise would have just laughed at the proposition of reading our Bibles.

Thirty days went by quickly. It was a funny thing how we four found ourselves sharing the things we were reading in the Bible. When we reconvened, our attitudes and ideas had shifted dramatically. Although Mr. Wilson had checked in with us during the thirty days, for the most part he stayed uninvolved and kept his comments to a minimum.

For me, those thirty days changed my life. I became excited about a God who cared for me. I began to see the Bible as a book of inspiration and love. Although I had been baptized a few years earlier, it wasn't until after this experience that I made a serious commitment to Jesus Christ.

The quiet influence of this Bible teacher affected the way in which I have lived my life. Although I never thanked him for his courageous act, I believe he saw the fruit of his labor in my changed actions and attitudes.

Thanks, Mr. Wilson, for being willing to reach out and touch the life of this high school freshman.

Carel (Sanders) Mountain writes from Redding, California, where she teaches nursing at Shasta College. She also serves as an adjunct faculty member at Pacific Union College in Angwin, California.

He Taught Six Rs

My dad, Homer Hobart Dever, started his teaching career when I was a year old. Although he taught for thirty-five years in schools in Ohio, Tennessee, and Georgia, I was the only student he taught all eight grades. I have often wondered how many people, other than those in home-schools, can claim to have had the same teacher for all eight years of grade school.

Being the teacher's daughter was a unique experience. However, because I attended small schools, I rarely felt the other students considered me the teacher's daughter in a negative way. My dad made everyone feel equal regardless of his or her scholastic or social abilities.

My dad was a quiet, but respected, teacher. Everyone knew that his word was law, and for the most part, few students disobeyed. In addition to the traditional "three Rs," my dad also taught us three more important Rs.

He taught respect. He made sure all students treated each other equally, regardless of their home background or religion. He joined us in our games on the playground, encouraging all to play together with a good spirit. We weren't allowed to make fun of classmates if they couldn't perform as well as we thought they should.

He taught responsibility. He expected us to do our best in all of our subjects. He also gave us chores to do around the school, requiring us to do our part in keeping the place neat and clean.

He taught reverence. His behavior in the classroom and at church worship services exemplified a life that reverenced God as his supreme Guide.

We began each school day with singing and a devotional thought. While not a great singer himself, my dad knew the importance of music for everyone. During these worships, we were directed to God and nature, learning lessons that pointed us toward heaven.

Students who went through my dad's classroom learned how to type, cook, sew, and garden. He believed our learning should not be confined solely to the pages of the prescribed textbooks.

Now retired, my dad has taken up a new way to touch the lives of students. Each year he selects several names from a list of student missionaries and writes to them wherever they are ministering in foreign fields. Each month he sends them letters filled with words of encouragement and bits of news about things that are happening back in the United States.

Thank you, Dad, for being my role model, both at home and in the classroom where you made sure I learned not only reading, 'riting, and 'rithmetic, but also respect, responsibility, and reverence.

Lorna Rae Dever writes from Mill Spring, North Carolina, where she is self-employed.

Help at Night

DONALD HARVEY

I was having a difficult time with some calculus problems. It was late, around 11:30 P.M., and I was about to give up solving a particular problem. Frustration had overwhelmed me to the point that I could not think logically anymore. After deciding to put my book away and go to bed, I had a crazy thought, "Why not call the teacher and get some help?"

It was the lateness of the hour and my frustration that drove me to such an irresponsible act. I picked up the phone and dialed the teacher's home number. The telephone rang six times, and then a low, sleepy voice on the other end said, "Hello?"

I paused a moment and contemplated hanging up. I knew I had awakened my teacher and was feeling both guilty and frightened at the prospect of meeting him the next day. Time seemed to drag by, and then I timidly said, "Dr. VanHorne, this is Don. I am sorry to call you so late, but I am having trouble with today's assignment." I paused and expected to hear him chastise me for calling and disturbing him so late at night. That is what I expected, but that is not what happened.

After a short pause, Dr. VanHorne said, "Oh, hi, Don. Let me get my book, and I'll help you with your problem." The way those words were said boosted my spirit and energized me to pursue solving the problem with renewed vigor. With the teacher's help, it was not long before the cloud of misunderstanding was lifted, and the problem was solved. I said

Goodbye in an appreciative way, and he assured me that I could call him any time I was having a problem.

After hanging up, I reflected on what had just happened. I told myself that if I was a teacher, I would want to be like Dr. VanHorne. At that time, I was not planning to go into teaching, but the experience that night left a lasting impression on my mind.

A few years later, I decided to pursue teaching, just for a year or two as a stepping stone to another career. The Lord, however, had other plans for me, and the "year or two" has turned into a career spanning more than three decades. The Lord knew I would enjoy teaching, so He allowed me to have experiences in my life that would help me relate to my own students.

Late one night, around 11:30 P.M., I got a call from a student. "Hello, Mr. Harvey. I am sorry to call you so late, but I don't understand how to solve the algebra problems you assigned us today. I have tried, but I just don't get it."

"Hi, Bill," I said. "Just a minute, let me get my book . . ."

Thanks, Dr. VanHorne, for the example you gave me of what a Christian teacher should be.

Donald Harvey writes from Madison, Tennessee, where he teaches science at Madison Academy. This incident happened in 1969 while he was a student at Kettering College of Medical Arts in Kettering, Ohio.

Hope Inspired Hope

MILDRED WHITE

Day after day she stood before our class of energetic teenagers, teaching us the basic Bible doctrines with certainty and imagination. I remember the day she drew word pictures of the Creation and Fall. Her face seemed to glow as she explained the meaning of the Bible verse we were to memorize—Genesis 3:15. She showed that the Fall wasn't the end because our Savior had come to this world to die to redeem us from this fallen state, and He was coming back again soon. There was hope and redemption for all of us, because He paid for our sins on the cross. Fascinated by what I heard, my heart stirred within me. This was my first year in an Adventist academy and my introduction to Hope Frisby, my Bible teacher and dean.

I had grown up in an Adventist home, but I rarely ever got to church because we lived out in the country far from any church family. I knew we were Adventists, but I didn't know why or what it meant. We didn't have worship or Bible study in our home, but my parents did cease their regular work on Sabbath. When I was in the tenth grade, I attended a public high school, and the world began to appear very attractive to me. I joined the popular crowd in having what I thought was a lot of fun.

Now, at seventeen, I found myself in the boarding academy at Canadian Union College, where I met Miss Frisby, the girls' dean and part-time Bible teacher. She was young, pretty, single, and most importantly, a loving and lovable Christian. As our dean, she was kind and gentle, but she could also be very firm. When she set up rules, we knew they were to be obeyed. In the worship sessions that she held in the girls' dorm, she taught us many things to help us become godly women—how to dress appropriately, the need for feminine hygiene, and about healthy relationships with boys.

However, it was as a Bible teacher that she had the greatest impact on my life. She taught us to memorize Scripture, including key texts for every lesson. I remember for one test we were required to know eighty Bible texts, and because of her diligence in teaching the importance of learning them, I knew everyone of them. Now many years later, I remember many of those texts and continue to memorize more.

I'll never forget the day she taught us the reason our church believes in the Spirit of prophecy as fulfilled in Ellen White. She explained the gift of prophecy with Bible texts and told us the experience of seventeen-year-old Ellen when she had her first vision and how God used her in a marvelous way to guide and direct this fledgling church. I had heard about Ellen White before, but only in discussion and arguments. Now I was so excited to learn this great truth. I couldn't wait to share it with my family and anyone who would listen!

In the spring of that school year, at an evening vesper program when a call was made to surrender to the Lord, I went forward to commit my life to Him in service. That was many, many years ago, and I have never looked back!

Thank you, Miss Frisby, for your faithful Christian witness.

Mildred J. White is a retired church school teacher living in Hayden, Idaho, where she continues to work with children.

How Creative Learning Affected My Life

AARON HALL

The most influential teacher in my life was Patricia Lynn Hall (Burton), my fifth-grade teacher at Willowbrook Adventist Junior Academy in Cumberland, Maryland. Mrs. Hall made learning fun and exciting in many ways. Even though I was a shy kid and didn't like school all that much, I left school each day with a smile because she made me feel that I was a special person.

I remember many activities she organized—dress-up days, pet days, battlefield tours, ski trips, choir performances, Christmas play productions, and other exciting things. Even though some of those trips and activities might sound non-educational, Mrs. Hall always found a way to make everything a learning experience.

The greatest impact Mrs. Hall had on my learning experience was when she announced that each of us would have the opportunity to help the church collect money for its Ingathering goal that year. Along with the church pastor, she organized after-school Ingathering trips to several different cities throughout the area. I was pretty nervous at first, because I really didn't like talking to people I didn't know. Reluctantly, I signed up for the outing.

Mrs. Hall split us up into several different groups, and we set out knocking on doors. Though I don't remember how much money I collected that day, I do remember having fun and how much I enjoyed trying something new. After we got back that first day, I decided I wanted to go help the church collect money every time I possibly could. I went every single time and collected more than a hundred dollars! That doesn't seem like a lot of money today, but as an eleven-year-old kid, I thought I had really accomplished something.

Looking back, I realize this activity had a huge impact on my life. I learned how to talk to people I didn't know without being terrified. I was also able to meet many people who weren't Christians and introduce them to God and the Seventh-day Adventist Church. This helped me get more involved with my church, even at a young age.

Mrs. Hall's impact on my life cannot be summed up in just this one experience. But I feel it best describes the effect that she had on my life while she was my teacher. I will always be grateful for all the creative learning experiences and support she gave me.

Aaron Hall writes from Keene, Texas.
He works as a billing clerk at Huguley
Hospital in Fort Worth, Texas.

I Owe, I Owe Mrs. O.!

Kathy Bollinger

She was a little Japanese firecracker with a wealth of diverse knowledge. And I, well, I was an Iowa farm girl, newly graduated from Union College in Nebraska, whose experience with diversity consisted mostly of recognizing various breeds of cattle and makes of tractors.

We met at San Gabriel Adventist Elementary in Southern California; I, an excited-beyond-belief first-grade teacher, and she, Mrs. Winifred Oshita, my school principal.

Mrs. O. was a tornado! She was everywhere—busy, busy, busy. Mrs. O. was an encyclopedia—knowledge, knowledge, knowledge. Mrs. O. was electricity—always turning on my thinking switch! Mrs. O. was a cheerleader—waving me on with enthusiasm! She was godly—pointing me daily to the Master Teacher. Mrs. O. was delightful and loved by her constituents. And lucky me—she was my mentor!

A first-year teacher with an excellent mentor is very fortunate, and I felt honored. But Mrs. O. had one quality, thoroughness, that was a thorn in my side. I wasn't used to exactness; a ballpark figure seemed OK to me. But Mrs. O. didn't believe in ballpark figures unless you were right on base. When I turned in my lesson plans each Thursday afternoon, she often gave them back to me Friday morning for correction before the weekend. That first year, I spent hours recopying my register because I had used red ink instead of black. (Aren't teachers supposed to be purveyors of red?) Long after the other teachers had left for the summer, I remained, phoning

60

the parents of all of my thirty-plus students to complete the "cumulative folders" with exact information right down to the correct spelling of parents' middle names. Nothing could be turned in unless it was correct.

I must admit I didn't have a smile on my face during those weeks, but I did learn to be precise. I learned that the value of a job well done emits an inner pride that can't be bought. I learned that "He that is faithful in that which is least is faithful also in much" (Luke 16:10). I learned that Mrs. O. was concerned not only with my outward teaching but also with my inner thoughts. From that year forward, I have looked at mundane paper work with a resolve to be thorough. I learned a lifelong lesson from that wonderful lady—my principal and my friend.

I owe you much, Mrs. O. Thanks!

Kathy (Hanson) Bollinger writes from Lincoln, Nebraska, where she is an associate professor of education at Union College.

La Señorita

LOWELL DUNSTON

I met La Señorita when I enrolled in Spanish class my junior year at Pacific Union College Preparatory School (PUC Prep). Shy though I was, I became her biggest challenge the first week of class. It was easy for her to find equivalent Spanish names for all the other students, but finding one for "Lowell" proved to be a major task. However, by the second week of class, she christened me "Lobito."

We dared not come to class unprepared, for we never knew on which intricate part of the lesson she might quiz us orally. When we were unprepared, she worked us over in class—an intense experience we did not wish to repeat. Yet there were no hard feelings. We understood that she wanted us to do our very best.

The highlight of the year was our annual Spanish field trip. It was a day of total immersion in the Spanish cultural history of California. We visited the Petaluma Adobe State Historic Park; the home of General Vallejo, territorial governor of California; and the Sonoma, San Rafael, and San Francisco missions. The grand finale of the day was dinner at Taco the Town in Vallejo.

La Señorita's commitment to her students did not end with class or field trips. On weekends she was chaperon for our teen excursions. Many a summer Sabbath she accompanied us to Armstrong Grove, organ concerts in San Francisco, or camping trips on the California coast. Returning home late one Saturday night, our group stopped at Vern's Drive-In in

62

St. Helena, the only fast-food place in the area. We had just ordered our vegeburgers when a carload of local high school toughs parked beside us. Tobacco smoke was purposely blown our way. Comments like "lettuce eaters" polluted the air. All of a sudden they spied La Señorita in the back seat. "We see you had to bring your Mama with you," shouted one of the toughs. Quick on the retort, one of us shouted back, "Yes, and she's the life of the party!" While La Señorita had the laugh of her life, our antagonists quietly vanished.

Four decades have come and gone. La Señorita is our only remaining high school teacher. She has graced our weddings and rarely missed a class reunion or alumni event. At eighty years of age, she still zooms the Los Angeles freeways, travels Europe, and keeps track of her students. This past summer, my wife and I had the privilege of taking her to breakfast. My family had just visited the California missions to relive treasured memories. As we shared photo memories on my laptop at the restaurant table, La Señorita stated that those years were among the happiest of her life.

La Señorita, Carol Dunn, bequeathed to her students lessons for life. We caught the spirit of pursuing excellence and the joy found in a life of service to our church and to our world. It's probably no accident that at least half of her Spanish class students have spent at least some years as teachers. We have found joy in passing on the torch of learning that La Señorita lit for each of us.

Lowell Dunston writes from Lynnwood, Washington, where he serves as principal at Cypress Adventist School.

Learning to Trust

I was five years old when I met Mrs. Katherine Meckling at Clara E.
Rogers Elementary School in College Place, Washington. I was starting
first grade, and she was my sister's second-grade teacher in the classroom
next door. I was afraid of being alone at school. Maybe it was because I
was a second child and not used to being alone. Or maybe it was because
my father was a professional ball player who was gone six months each
year, but Mrs. Meckling understood.

Every morning, for a long time, I could not be consoled until my
teacher brought Mrs. Meckling from the classroom next door to comfort
me. Mrs. Meckling's sweet words, her encircling arms, and gentle way
always calmed me. Often she would just talk to me, but some days she
would take me to her classroom, where I could see my sister from the
doorway. Whatever she did, she always calmed my heart. She also took
that opportunity to teach me two Bible verses, "Lo, I am with you alway,
even unto the end of the world" (Matthew 28:20), and "I will never
leave thee, nor forsake thee" (Hebrews 13:5). These verses have been
important to me all my life. She taught me that I never have to be afraid
of being alone, because Jesus will never leave me.

One sunny day while I was still in the first grade, I was playing inside
the bars on the merry-go-round during recess when I lost my footing
and fell under the seats, banging my face on the bench and then falling
out onto the ground. I came up crying—with a bloody nose and a

wiggly tooth. I ran past the playground monitor and into the school to find Mrs. Meckling. She gathered me up in her arms and took me into the bathroom where she washed my face, dusted off my clothes, and exclaimed, "Oh, now you have a real wiggly tooth! What shall we do with this one?"

It was my first loose tooth, and she made it fun instead of scary. She helped me look into the mirror and see it dangling in my mouth. I trusted her so much that I let her pull it out! After that, I let her pull two others that she put in an envelope for me to take home for the tooth fairy. She was the first person outside of my family I learned to trust. Because she was loving, and because she loved God and spoke of Him so well, it was an easy transition for me to learn to love and trust Him, too.

A few years later, our Bible teacher frightened us with dark stories of the "time of trouble," but I was already grounded in a knowledge of a loving God, and I knew Jesus would be with me, that His Spirit would never leave me, and that if I kept my heart connected to Him, I never, ever needed to be afraid.

During my senior year in academy, I was social vice-president in charge of a large banquet, yet I had no faculty adviser who knew about decorating. I went to find Mrs. Meckling, who was then teaching in the education department at Walla Walla College, and asked for her help. She drove me to a craft warehouse where I could dream big decorating dreams and buy supplies at bargain rates. Then without reimbursement, just because she was my friend, she taught us girls to make centerpieces and to decorate and plan for large gatherings.

3—A. T. T. H.

When we girls were in college, Mrs. Meckling took classes to become a wedding coordinator. She was always looking for ways to delight us in the Lord, and my wedding day was no exception. At the end of the wedding ceremony, as my new husband and I turned around to leave the sanctuary, we looked up and saw Mrs. Meckling in the back of the Walla Walla College Church. She came rushing down the aisle, motioning for us to hurry! When she caught up with us, we ran back toward the narthex together as she told us how God had put His bow in a cloudless sky on a sunny July evening in order to show us that He would be with us forever. He would never leave us or forsake us. And there spanning the sky of my hometown was a beautiful rainbow of promise! Mrs. Meckling never forgot how important it was for me to be connected—and neither did God.

Lou (Kinzer) Blanchfield, Ph.D., writes from Churdan, Iowa, where she works as an education consultant and writes grant proposals.

Lost the Battle, but Won the War

ALANE BRITT

I shivered—not from the cold, but from apprehension—as I sat on the closed toilet-seat lid and wrapped my arms tighter around my drawn-up legs. Would "she" find me?

"She" was my archenemy, the woman who made my eight-year-old existence miserable. "She" made me do unbelievable things—like stay after school and do extra homework while everyone else got to play as they waited for the bus or take homework home at nights and on weekends. Nobody else had to do such things—only me! She hated me; I just knew it.

"She," my third-grade teacher, Mrs. Barlow, had the audacity to say that I couldn't read and to think she could make a difference. I couldn't read, but so what! Obviously, reading was overrated or I wouldn't have made it to the third grade.

As the bathroom door creaked open and I watched black canvas shoes walk into the stall beside me, my body tensed. The toilet lid closed. The shoes disappeared. Resignation replaced my apprehension. Suddenly a very tired face appeared over the top of the stall. "Come back to the room, Alane," Mrs. Barlow said quietly.

After I had followed her into the classroom, she said with resignation, "You can go out and play with the others, Alane." She looked defeated, and my spirits soared because I thought I had won the battle. She realized that her current strategy couldn't defeat me. Elation filled my little soul as I rushed out to play with the others. I had won the battle! Or had I?

The next afternoon, following my "victory," I was invited to stay after school, bring my reading book, and sit in the "reading chair" beside Mrs. Barlow's desk, where we read together and studied phonics. For several weeks, Mrs. Barlow and I met after school to read. These sessions led to trips to the library with my family. I carried stacks of books home and finished reading them before our next weekly visit. Mrs. Barlow's tutoring enabled me to "test out" of my senior year of high school English and take a college English 101 class instead. I also was able to bypass the college literature requirement for my nursing degree!

As I reflect on my life, I know my success as an army nurse, taking care of our brave soldiers, can be attributed to three things—my Lord, who leads me daily; my parents, who supported me; and Mrs. Betty Barlow, who taught me to love reading. She may have lost a battle that day, but she definitely won the war!

Alane Britt writes from Hawaii,
where she is stationed as a
nurse in the U.S. Army.

Mastering Modern Math

JOHN LOOR JR.

In the fall of 1963, my father accepted a call to pastor a church in the La Sierra, California, area. That was an intimidating move for me! I moved from a small school with about ten students in my eighth-grade class to La Sierra Demonstration School with sixty-five students in the class. With so many eighth-graders, we had to be divided into two rooms. Not only was my eighth-grade class large, the program was departmentalized with the seventh- and eighth-grade classes together—something new for me.

Since the elementary school was a demonstration school for La Sierra College education students, our curriculum reflected the latest trends. Besides being my homeroom teacher, Mr. Roland Rhynus was also my math teacher. He taught a class titled "Concepts of Modern Math," which, for the life of me, I could not understand! Noticing my struggles, he came to me one day and said, "Why don't you come to my home in the evening, and I'll give you some extra help."

Since we lived in the same neighborhood, I rode my bike to Mr. Rhynus's house around suppertime several times a week. He took his precious time when he could have been with his family to help this struggling math student understand the concepts I was not grasping in class. Mr. Rhynus was an excellent teacher; and in a few weeks I caught up with the class.

Because of his patient teaching, the fundamentals I learned that year stayed with me through my academy and college math courses. I received excellent grades in academy algebra. And, when I took my algebra class in college, I remember specifically thinking that the reason I was earning an A in the class was because of Mr. Rhynus. The unselfish gift of his personal time to help me grasp the concepts of modern math represented Jesus to me and will never be forgotten.

John R. Loor Jr. writes from Bozeman, Montana, where he serves as president of the Montana Conference of Seventh-day Adventists.

Math Lesson

RUTH LENZ

Zero period!

What an awful time to have to think about math—especially senior math! But, wanting to become a math teacher myself, I was pleased that our math teacher, Mr. Ken Dunlap, was willing to get up so early to offer a senior math course to us dedicated students before regular classes began for the day.

As I remember that morning, Mr. Dunlap was explaining to us the concept of infinity—a number that extends forever. Early in the morning, we sometimes had a difficult time grasping hard-to-understand ideas, but he cheerfully and patiently explained each of our questions. Suddenly, right in the middle of the discussion, he turned out the lights, leaving the basement classroom very dark, as it was just dawning outside.

"Turn around," he urged. "I just can't continue teaching when so much beauty is right behind you." As we turned our chairs around, we beheld the most beautiful sunrise I have ever seen. We spent the rest of the class period with the lights out discussing infinity as it related to eternity. The increasing glow from the gradually rising sun slowly filled the classroom. "Heaven is so important," he concluded, "that you should let nothing get in the way of each of you being there."

I'm sure I learned a lot of math from Mr. Dunlap that year that helped me prepare for my career as a teacher. But that morning, when he took the time to talk to us about our future with Jesus, was the most important class period I ever had.

Ruth Lenz writes from Spokane, Washington, where she teaches math, science, and Bible at Spokane Junior Academy.

Modeling an Unselfish Life

SHELLEY ANN BACON

For me, 1979 was a memorable year. In August, I was married to my best friend, Barry, and three weeks later we began our last year at Union College. I was studying education, and Barry was headed to medical school after completing his undergraduate degree in religion.

Both Barry and I were finishing college in three years. I was allowed to pursue this aggressive educational path because one of my professors believed I could do it. This professor had already inspired me with her knowledge and wit during my first class under her tutelage—Psychology of Human Growth and Development. But what most impressed me was her philosophy of education, that driving force behind who she was as an educator.

She believed learning was more important than the amount of time it took to learn, and she demonstrated that philosophy by allowing students the opportunity to improve their grades by retaking tests. She believed in making class content important to her students and acted on that philosophy by creating fascinating classes filled with examples, stories, demonstrations, discussions, and wonderful learning.

As I started my student teaching during the first semester of my senior year, she wrote encouraging notes on my evaluations and helped me see my potential as a teacher. When my father died suddenly and unexpectedly in December, she made sure there were flowers at the funeral from Union College and the George Stone School where I was teaching. She was the perfect role model for me as a future educator.

As I began my senior year, the education department was making plans to take the education majors to a conference in Atlanta, Georgia. The cost of the trip would be eighty dollars, a mere pittance today, but a huge amount in 1979 to a newlywed couple living on Barry's income from a part-time construction job. We discussed the financial commitment and decided that if we put aside just a few dollars each week from our grocery money, we could have enough saved by the deadline. Every few weeks, I took twenty dollars to the education office and put it toward the trip. Finally, I had the entire eighty dollars in my account in time to attend the conference.

Shortly before the trip date, we received a call from Barry's sister-in-law. Barry's parents were to celebrate their twenty-fifth wedding anniversary that summer. All the siblings were expected to contribute a hundred dollars toward the gift of a chandelier for their dining room. Where were we going to get that kind of money? There was only one logical place—from my trip fund. I reluctantly went to the education office and asked for my money back.

Just a few days later, I received a call from the education office. I was approved to go on the education trip. How can this be? I queried. There must be some mistake. Didn't the person remember that I had withdrawn my funds? I couldn't possibly come up with eighty dollars at this late date.

"Your account is all paid up," the person told me. "Someone has anonymously paid your way." Through some deductive reasoning and a few clues, I figured out who the donor must be—none other than my favorite professor.

The memories of the conference are a blur in my mind today. But the memory of the dedication, the example, the love of that wonderful woman who took time not only to teach me things related to educating precious children for God, but also to model the power of an unselfish life, will live with me forever.

Thank you, Dr. Virginia Simmons, from the bottom of my heart.

Shelley Ann (Dickinson) Bacon writes from Colville, Washington, where she teaches sophomore humanities subjects and pre-algebra for Adventist Education for the 21st Century, a virtual classroom sponsored by the Florida Conference.

Mr. Nick

ANNI HISEY

I've always been sort of a nerd. Well, maybe not even "sort of."
Probably "definitely." Nowhere was this more apparent than in grade
school. My unique combination of grown-up humor, excessively large
vocabulary (due to being an only child and having adults as playmates),
and the tendency to gloat was likely to blame for my estrangement from
the "cool" kids.

When I entered Cape Ferello Adventist School in the middle of my
second-grade year, I hoped to change my previous reputation as a weirdo
and fit right in. Unfortunately, when there are only eight other students in
your school (Brookings, Oregon, is not a booming metropolis) and you try
a little too hard, it's easy to be labeled right from the start. Such was the
case with me.

I'm sure the kids were nice enough, but making friends with an
emotionally charged seven-year-old with fresh baggage from her parents'
nasty divorce can be challenging. Most of the kids decided they had
better things to do than take time getting to be my friend. That would
have been OK if they'd left it at that. But when kids get bored at recess,
they need someone to tease, and I became an easy target. I cried easily
and got mad in an instant, providing my fellow classmates with endless
opportunities for fun.

That's when I discovered the wonders of staying inside during recess
to hang out with my teacher, Mr. Dan Nickolatos, while a teacher's aide

supervised the other students on the playground. I loved going with him to his greenhouse to pick raspberries. Mr. Nick, as we called him, was a naturalist at heart and loved showing me amazing things—such as how strong a spider web could be or the way the vines grew in their pots. He would ask how things were with me and compassionately listen as I told him of my parents' fighting or he would just divert my attention to something beautiful. Whatever he did, he made me feel valuable. Every morning he greeted me with a grand smile, a shoulder-crushing squeeze, and an enthusiastic, "Hi, Anni!" I knew I could count on him for support, encouragement, and sometimes to be my surrogate dad when mine was miles away in southern California.

Another thing I admired was his dedication to God and old-fashioned religion. Every Friday before AJY (remember those meetings?), he would bring out the songbook and sit and play any song we could sing. I'm amazed at how he motivated us to sing with all our hearts. Somehow we didn't care who was "cool" when we were having worship. Mr. Nick made worship about God and His awesome love for us. He showed by example what it meant to be a Christian.

Mr. Nick went above and beyond what a teacher is expected to do. He had four kids of his own and a full life without having lonely students to mentor, but he was never too busy for me. I was invited to the Nickolatos house for many Friday nights and Sabbath lunches. They made me feel as though I was one of their own children. Kathy, his wife, was the perfect hostess and always made sure I was as comfortable as could be. Their openness and love was exactly what I needed in order to feel that I did, indeed, have a place in this world.

I think it's because of Mr. Nick's strong faith in a loving God and the way he put his faith into action that I'm a teacher today. I learned many facts and interesting things in his classes, but what affected me the most was how Mr. Nick taught me to see past outward appearances and appreciate eternal things.

Anni J. Hisey writes from Wenatchee, Washington, where she teaches at Cascade Christian Academy.

Mrs. Prewitt's Sacrifice

JENNIFER WOEHLER

I will never forget my sixth-grade teacher, Mrs. Vivian Prewitt. It all began in August 1989, when the fog cleared enough to allow the Alaska Airlines plane to land, bringing Mrs. Prewitt to Nome, Alaska—a remote town with a population of roughly four thousand.

Mrs. Prewitt temporarily left her husband and home in Fairbanks, Alaska, to dedicate a year of her life to teaching five rambunctious students. Her students included a tall, seventh-grade boy with a sense of humor; myself, a shy but mischievous sixth-grader; a strong-willed fifth-grade girl with a fiery temper; my brother, a talkative fourth-grader; and a quiet, but spunky, third-grade girl who knew how to put the boys in their place.

Mrs. Prewitt specialized in making boring subjects—like handwriting and social studies—fun and relevant. In the fall of that year, when the Iron Curtain began to crumble, Mrs. Prewitt asked our neighbor, Joe Davis, if he would take a photo album over to Russia for us when he traveled there, so that Russian kids could see what Nome was like. We spent hours riding around in Mrs. Prewitt's car taking pictures for the album. We photographed rusty gold dredges, the rock seawall along Front Street, and the Iditarod finish-line marker. We also wrote letters to Russian kids. The girl I wrote to was from Provideniya, on the Siberian coast.

Our small, one-room classroom required flexibility and creativity, which Mrs. Prewitt readily displayed. The students competed against each other in map drills and games to learn about geography. Because of Mrs. Prewitt's influence, I loved geography and later participated in the state-level National Geographic Geography Bee. Sometimes Mrs. Prewitt took us ice skating at a nearby pond for recess. During the stormy winter months, we often played basketball, bowled, and made gymnastic pyramids at the recreation center downtown, since we didn't have our own gym.

We made sure Mrs. Prewitt never had a dull moment in her classroom. The other students walked home for lunch, since they lived just a few blocks away. My brother, Jeff, and I couldn't go home for lunch, but Mrs. Prewitt trusted us to eat our lunches at school while she ate at her house next door. Most of the time, we were trustworthy. But one day, Mrs. Prewitt returned from lunch to find an empty classroom. She searched high and low, inside and out. We smiled smugly from our hiding places when we heard her calling our names.

Pretty soon the storage shed door opened with a loud *Cre-e-e-e-a-a-k!* I shivered with excitement, wondering what our punishment would be. Suddenly, I heard Mrs. Prewitt exclaim sternly, "Rob!" The shed erupted with laughter as Rob dropped from his upside-down position hanging from the rafters. Soon, Jeff burst from his hiding place among the extra desks, Sara crawled out from behind some tables, and Anna and I slithered from behind a stack of chairs. Mrs. Prewitt could have punished us severely, but she scolded us mildly and joined in the laughter. She put up with our pranks in a lighthearted manner that we soon grew to love.

When the year was over, none of us found it very easy to say goodbye. When Mrs. Prewitt made a classroom video to demonstrate her teaching skills, we tried to act goofy so no one else would want to hire her and we'd get to keep her.

I kept in touch with Mrs. Prewitt for many years. As a college student, my memory of Mrs. Prewitt's creative, enthusiastic teaching played a role in inspiring me to become a teacher. And guess where I taught my first year? Nome, Alaska. By that time, because church members and teachers like Mrs. Prewitt wouldn't let it die, the school had three classrooms and more than thirty students. She sacrificed her time with her own family for our seemingly insignificant school and affected my life forever. That's why Mrs. Prewitt will always remain one of my most memorable teachers.

Jennifer (Downs) Woehler writes from Caldwell, Idaho, where she is currently a fifth- and sixth-grade teacher assistant at Caldwell Adventist Elementary School.

My Favorite Elementary Teacher

Ron Scott

My fourth-grade teacher, Miss Edith Fitch, was an outstanding person. Born with only about 15 percent of normal hearing, she could not hear bells, whistles, or much of human speech. She understood what people were saying to her mostly by lip reading. My classmates and I didn't know any of this when we were in her classroom. All we knew was that she was difficult to understand because of a speech impediment called "deaf speech." But we quickly became accustomed to it. She managed to keep her secret even from her students' parents.

The first hint my parents had that Miss Fitch was hearing impaired was when she and a teacher friend spent a couple of weeks sharing an apartment with our family while we conducted a couple of Vacation Bible Schools in the remote northern community of Yellowknife, Northwest Territories, Canada. One morning, my father spoke to Miss Fitch while she was washing dishes, and she didn't respond. He wondered if she had been offended and asked the other teacher about it. She told him Miss Fitch probably had not heard, because she was deaf. Even then, my parents did not recognize the extent of her deafness.

In the classroom, Miss Fitch sat facing us at all times and was very alert to students talking or moving about. We listened to an educational radio program every week at the same time. None of us realized she couldn't hear it, so we were not inspired at the time by her triumph over hardship, nor were we tempted to trick her by talking behind her back, whispering, or engaging in other inappropriate communication. On one occasion, she kept her class working through a fire alarm, but was able to apologize without blowing her cover. Even her colleagues had no idea of the handicap she was dealing with.

Since I wasn't aware of her deafness at the time, the reason I remember Miss Fitch is for her kindness, understanding, and generosity. On a science test she gave, we were asked to explain why a kite flies. My explanation must have been thorough because she gave me extra points on the question, bringing my test score over 100 percent. It was a real boost to me because I lacked self-confidence at that age. I had never really excelled at anything and was not well accepted by my peers. Miss Fitch helped me see that science was a field I could excel in, and from then on, I felt confident of my abilities.

Another incident I remember was when Miss Fitch gave a spelling test of a hundred words or so. The words gradually increased in difficulty as the test progressed. At the end of the test, she announced the names of three students who had scored significantly higher than grade level. I was one of those three, and that recognition also felt good. On a later spelling test, I wrote something like "Injun" for "engine," probably as a joke, but she gave me 100 percent, writing, "I know you know how to spell this word." She insisted on students doing their best.

I had other excellent teachers in junior high, high school, and college. I'm sure several of them influenced my decision to become a teacher and may also have helped direct me to the field of science, but Miss Fitch is the first such influence I am aware of. And her influence did not stop in grade four. I recall the summer twelve years later, just before I began teaching, when I was taking Adventist Church History in summer school. Miss Fitch was also taking the course to upgrade her certification. At the end of the class, I told her that having her sit behind me in class helped me keep my focus, despite the heat, the distraction of summer activities going on outdoors, and the somewhat monotonous presentation in the classroom. She responded by telling me that I had likewise pushed her to do her best because she couldn't bear the thought of coming in behind a former student!

Though Miss Fitch is retired from the classroom, she still volunteers in the Canadian University College historical archives. When I go there, I make a point of speaking with her. We share stories and memories, and I always come away feeling uplifted.

Thanks, Miss Fitch.

Ron Scott writes from Hubbards, Nova Scotia, Canada, where he teaches science at Sandy Lake Academy.

My First American Teacher

BETTINA BUTENKO

When I think about which Adventist teacher has most influenced my life, Ms. Rose Graham comes to my mind instantly. She was my fourth-grade teacher at Ruth Murdoch Elementary School in Berrien Springs, Michigan.

I came to the United States from the little country of Denmark, in Europe. I barely knew how to speak English, let alone how to spell or write the language. I had left my friends and favorite teacher behind and was now starting a new and different life with my family in America.

Although I was very nervous and frightened my first day of school, it turned out to be a wonderful day because I couldn't have gotten a better teacher. Ms. Graham was so sweet and caring toward all her students. There were quite a few students who didn't know much English in her class, but she was always very patient and willing to help us with everything.

One of the things I remember most about her teaching was that she had us memorize Bible passages. We would memorize little by little, straight from the Bible. We not only learned memory verses, but we also learned to sing the Ten Commandments and the three angels' messages. We even memorized Isaiah 53 and recited it at churches. I remember one student memorized Martin Luther King's "I Have a Dream" speech.

When I look back, I realize how much it helped us to become better students to memorize those passages. Day by day, my English got better, and after a few months I was getting good grades in all my subjects, as if English were my native language.

Even though we did do a lot of work, we also had a lot of fun at school. All of us learned how to knit our own pillows—even the boys. At Thanksgiving we had a mini-Thanksgiving dinner, in which we dressed up as Pilgrims and Indians. It made the holidays something fun and exciting to look forward to.

From time to time, on weekends, Ms. Graham had us participate in Benton Harbor Street Ministries, where we would sing and play music at the local nursing home. Seeing how happy this made the people had a great impact on my life. It made ministering fun. When we finished singing, Ms. Graham would take us to her house, where we would make cookies together.

Not only was Ms. Graham our teacher, she was also our friend. If we needed to talk, she was there for us. You really felt she cared and wanted to help.

We were Ms. Graham's last class; she retired at the end of the 1998–1999 school year. I am privileged to have had her as my teacher. She is the one person in my life who really showed me what a Christian should be like.

Bettina Butenko is a student at Andrews Academy in Berrien Springs, Michigan.

My Highway Mentor

In the spring of 1979, I was a freshman elementary education major at Union College in Lincoln, Nebraska, unsure whether I wanted to stay in education. Our education club planned a trip to Denver, Colorado, to visit various schools that were known for their progressive curriculum and teaching techniques. The trip was great, as we were able to observe first-hand what we had been reading about in our education course textbook. Dr. Chuck Felton, education department chairman, was one of the sponsors on that trip.

Our plan was to spend the last afternoon at a particular school and then head back to Lincoln; however, our visit went longer than planned. Leaving late, plus losing one hour due to the time change, we wouldn't arrive back at the college until very early the next morning. We had two vehicles and three drivers. Dr. Felton volunteered to drive one vehicle all the way back with no relief, while the other two drivers switched off in the second vehicle.

I had the privilege of sitting in the front seat and talking to Dr. Felton all the way back to Lincoln in order to keep him awake. We talked of family, school news, current issues, and other topics of interest. After several miles of small talk, I asked Dr. Felton why he became an educator, hoping he would share his experience. Dr. Felton, always slow and deliberate in his response to important questions, began to talk with me about his calling to serve the Lord in whatever capacity He directed.

Dr. Felton told of his days in Africa, the challenges and the experience for his growing family. He shared the highlights of being principal of Oak Park Academy in Nevada, Iowa, and the rewarding experience of influencing the lives of his students. He brought each experience to life and shared how the Lord led him in his service to the church.

The travel time flew by, and before long we could see the lights of Lincoln framed by the faint glow of the rising eastern sun. Tired but energized, I thought about all the things Dr. Felton had shared in our five-hundred mile conversation. I determined, that early morning, I wanted to be an educator and leader like Dr. Felton.

Since that rich encounter, I have served the church in various capacities as a teacher and administrator and have tried to pattern my service after that of Dr. Felton's. I have traveled full circle and currently serve as the chairman of the Division of Human Development at Union College, the very position once occupied by Dr. Charles E. Felton—my highway mentor.

Joseph R. Allison, Ed.D., writes from Lincoln, Nebraska, where he serves as chair of the Division of Human Development at Union College.

My Lifelong Hero

JACK PARNELL

In 1939 during the Great Depression, I was fourteen years old as I entered my sophomore year of high school at the Birmingham Junior Academy. Stanley Harris was my tenth-grade teacher. His teaching credentials were just short of a Ph.D. The pay was sixty-five dollars per month, and there were no other subsidies. Professor Harris and his wife, Vaughtie, got an apartment in an Adventist home with the Smiths. The Harrises shared a kitchen and economized in every possible way.

Algebra was one of my new subjects. I had always been very good in arithmetic, but this new-fangled algebra was worse than Greek to me. I struggled for a few days with no improvement. I then told my Mother, "I am going to quit algebra."

She said, "No, you are not going to quit."

I said, "Well, Henry Starnes quit."

She countered, "But you are not Henry Starnes."

My mother called Professor Harris at the Smith house and asked if he could spend some time tutoring me the next Sunday morning. That two-hour session helped, so a second two-hour session was arranged for the next Sunday. Suddenly, a light dawned! I was off and running.

I went on to take high school geometry, second-year algebra, and trigonometry. In college, I had a double major in physics and mathematics. At the University of Tennessee, I took every math course in the undergraduate catalogue. My physics professor worked to get me

89

a teaching fellowship at the University of North Carolina, where I also took additional graduate courses in mathematics and physics. I received a master's degree in physics.

My first job out of graduate school was at the Naval Ordnance Laboratory in White Oak, Maryland, where I was immediately put in charge of the mathematics program for developing a classified, rocket-fired, anti-submarine weapon. Two years later, I pursued my love of flying. I went on to become a professional pilot, instrument flight instructor, aviation accident investigator, and an FAA-designated pilot examiner. Without those tutoring sessions from Professor Harris, my technical education would have ended because mathematics has been foundational for my entire life's work!

Professor Harris later became a well-known pastor and evangelist. My family kept in touch with him as long as he lived. We visited in each other's homes, recalling my problems with algebra and his great influence on my life. Elder Harris has been a lifelong hero to me.

Jack L. Parnell writes from
Collegedale, Tennessee.

My Most Valuable Lesson

Rusty Litten

When I reflect back on the many different educators I had during elementary school, academy, college, and university, one stands out above all the others: Helmut "Chuck" Liers.

Mr. Liers was the manager of Shenandoah Valley Academy's bindery from 1956 to 1971. During that time, the bindery was the major moneymaking business at SVA. Roland John, one of SVA's former business managers, said Mr. Liers was so frugal and would research needs for the bindery so completely that when he made a request of the school board, the board gave him anything he wanted.

"Rusty, this is how it is done in the 'Old Country,' " was a phrase I heard many times in my two-and-a-half years of working in the bindery. Both of Mr. Liers's parents were from Germany. I remember one day, as I was gluing back strips on books, Mr. Liers came by and told me I could get more done by using a different brush. I told him I thought my way was the faster way. He challenged me to a race to see who could do the most in a ten-minute period. Needless to say, at the end of ten minutes, I began to use a different brush.

Besides teaching me the importance of working hard, Mr. Liers also emphasized the importance of working smartly and efficiently. He seemed to be everywhere, showing students a better, quicker, or more efficient way to do their different bindery tasks. He was always around to keep me from spending too much time at the drinking fountain.

I believe that Helmut "Chuck" Liers taught me one of the most valuable lessons I ever learned—the importance of knowing how to work.

Thank you, Mr. Liers.

Lowell Sidney Russell (Rusty) Litten worked for Mr. Liers in the SVA bindery from 1959 to 1962. Rusty writes from Orlando, Florida, where he teaches at Orlando Junior Academy.

My Summer of Disbelief

LYNDON FURST

It was the summer of 1969, and American higher education was in a state of ferment. I was attending the University of the Pacific in California's central valley, pursuing an advanced degree in educational administration. Most of my previous education had been in the relatively safe environment of Adventist schools. While the University of the Pacific is a Methodist institution, it was essentially secular in most aspects of its operation. None of the faculty I encountered gave allegiance to religion of any kind.

A professor of sociology was particularly hostile to religion and especially to Christianity. In his lectures each day, he found some way to disparage religious belief. Periodically, he launched into tirades against Christians, who, according to him, were responsible for all the injustice in the world. In his more rational moments, the professor was quite convincing. He could marshal a mountain of factual evidence to show that the Christian faith was truly the "opiate of the masses." Doubt began to cloud my mind, as I had to admit that he was correct in much of what he said.

Nothing in my previous education had prepared me for this experience. My undergraduate studies at Emmanuel Missionary College had been based on a simple faith in the Bible and Ellen White. Higher-order thinking about religion was not part of the curriculum in those days. Doubt and skepticism were to be kept to oneself. So the learned professor at the University of the Pacific had a distinct advantage in the game he played with my mind.

In some ways I found the experience exhilarating. All of us have doubts about our faith at one time or another, and for the first time I found it safe to express them. Graduate education teaches one to be skeptical of ideas that are based primarily on emotion, and as I applied the processes of rational thought that I was learning, I had to admit that there were not many solid arguments for the validity of Christian belief.

My father, who had encouraged me in pursuing advanced education, had warned me that it would be easy to lose my faith if I was not careful. I would not give up the faith of a lifetime quickly. But logic dictated that I should. It was a long, hot summer and one of intense mental agony for me as I wrestled with this challenge to my beliefs. I did not want to give up my faith, but could see no rational reason to keep it either.

I have never been much of a believer in the mystical moment, but that is exactly what happened in that summer of spiritual doubt. One day while walking on campus, as I struggled with my dilemma, an old familiar tune began playing in my head. It brought me back to my days at Mt. Ellis Academy. The boys' dean had decided that our repertoire of worship songs was quite limited, and he encouraged us to learn some new ones. Every week he introduced a new song to us during evening worship. It was the tune and words of one of those songs that came to my mind some fifteen years later that helped me resolve the struggle I was enduring.

> I know not how this saving faith
> To me He did impart,
> Nor how believing in His Word
> Wrought peace within my heart.

These words, written by Daniel Webster Whittle in 1883 and set to music by James McGranahan, could have been written especially for me that summer. And the chorus gave special direction to my tortured mind:

> But I know Whom I have believéd,
> And am persuaded that He is able
> To keep that which I've committed
> Unto Him against that day.

There are some things, I concluded, that we know only because we know. They are not known by rational process, but by faith alone. When I realized that the rules of science were not appropriate to matters of faith, my lifelong faith in God was affirmed. My professor lost the battle for my soul, and hope was greatly strengthened.

I am thankful to God for the ministry of that boys' dean, Wesley Parker, who made a distinct impression on my life. Neither of us knew at the time that simply introducing a new song for evening worship would play such a pivotal part in my faith development.

"For this reason I also suffer these things; nevertheless I am not ashamed, for I know whom I have believed and am persuaded that He is able to keep what I have committed to Him until that day" (2 Timothy 1:12, NKJV).

Lyndon G. Furst, Ed.D., writes from Berrien Springs, Michigan, where he serves at Andrews University as dean of the School of Graduate Studies and professor of educational administration and supervision in the School of Education.

My Treasured Trophy

April was a very busy month for us eighth-graders and our teacher.
We were close to graduation and had back-to-back awards programs. One
week we had Science Fair Awards Day to recognize and pass out awards
for those students with outstanding science projects. Since I was in eighth
grade, I always helped our teacher, Mrs. Celia (Douglas) Levy, prepare
and pass out the awards. We worked hard laying out the awards just right
so there would be no interruptions or mistakes when they were passed
out. We announced each award according to grade level, starting with the
kindergarten students.

When it was time for the eighth-graders to receive their awards, Mrs.
Levy told me to go first, so I could get my medal and come back and
finish passing out the rest of the awards as she called out the names. Just as
the last person was called, we saw that we had run out of medals. Without
thinking much about it, I told Mrs. Levy she could give my medal to the
last student. As I quickly took off my medal and gave it to the student, I
didn't think it was that big of a deal. But Mrs. Levy did.

After the program, Mrs. Levy went through every classroom looking
for the missing medal. She discovered one of the kindergarteners who was
supposed to receive a certificate had received a medal instead. She brought
the medal and placed it around my neck herself.

As Honors Day approached, I knew I would not be receiving an award,
because I had not gotten on the honor roll at all that year. I had tried

96

hard, but no matter how hard I tried, my grades were not good enough. I also knew I would not receive a citizenship award, because I hadn't been at the school long enough to qualify. (I had only recently transferred back to this school from another school so I could graduate with my original classmates.) I prepared myself for the program by saying, "It's no big deal. You don't need an award to know you're smart."

At the Honors Day program, I helped Mrs. Levy pass out awards as usual. I also reminded myself that not receiving an award was no big deal. I would get one next time. Once again we started with the kindergarteners and ended with the eighth-graders. When my class came up, I flushed with embarrassment. No matter what I told myself, my feelings were hurt; I wanted an award, too. It hurt to be the only student in my class to receive absolutely nothing.

After receiving their awards, my classmates posed for the cameras as their proud parents took their pictures. I watched, wishing I could be included. After everyone had returned to their seats, Mrs. Levy told the crowd, "I have one last award." She proceeded to tell the crowd how I had given up my medal the week before and how much it meant to her. Tears flowed from my eyes, I was so happy to know someone did care. As I stood there listening and watching, Mrs. Levy pulled out a big trophy that read:

To: Sydney Reynolds for your act of kindness
From: Celia Levy, teacher.

As she handed me the trophy, she gave me the biggest hug any teacher could give. I couldn't help but smile the rest of the day. No one had ever shown me the kindness Mrs. Levy showed me that day. To this day I sleep with that trophy right over my head.

Mrs. Levy truly is one of the best teachers I have had. There were so many times when I felt that my whole world was coming to an end, but Mrs. Levy was always there for me. I am so grateful for the positive impact she has had on my life.

Sydney Reynolds writes from Birmingham, Alabama, where she is a tenth-grader at Ephesus Junior Academy.

My Very Best Teacher

A teacher that has greatly influenced my academic life is Mrs. Fran Haper. For the four years that I had her in elementary school, she encouraged me academically and taught me history and writing far beyond my grade levels at that time.

She made history interesting by making it interactive. One day, when we were learning about the Great Depression, we went to school and found that our desks and lockers were gone and that lunch was a soup kitchen. She said, "Welcome to the Great Depression." Another time, when we were learning about the Middle Ages, she hired two swordsmen to fight in our gym. When we studied about monks, we dressed up as monks and imitated their services. Through these intense and fun interactions, I learned history as never before and had a great time doing it.

She also made history fundamental. Her lectures were not only to the point, but interesting. She had a passionately strong political view, which caught the interest of us all. Her heroes were Rush Limbaugh and former president George Bush, and her motto was, "pushing back the frontiers of ignorance." She actually inspired me to start an online column called the "Global Conservative."

Mrs. Haper inspired my writing by believing in me. Repeatedly, she told me that one day I would write something great. To me writing was just a hobby, but to her it was much more. Her writing exercises, although sometimes difficult, prepared me not just for high school but for college. She had us write political columns, creative writing, and personal narratives. I appreciated her keen knowledge and ways of motivating us. Now, as I look back on assignments that seemed ridiculously difficult at the time, I find that they caused me to grow mentally, academically, and spiritually. If it were not for Mrs. Haper, I may not have the passions I do now.

I doubt I will ever have a teacher as good as Mrs. Haper, but I am thankful that I had her for as long as I did. The things that she taught me I know for sure I will use in my future. I thank her for giving me the fundamentals necessary for life.

Destin Michael Hebert is a junior at Bass Memorial Academy in Lumberton, Mississippi.

One Year That Changed My Life

A new teacher was coming! Our recently arrived pastor's wife had agreed to teach grades seven to ten in our church school. As a tenth-grader, I wasn't very hopeful. My school experience up to that point had not been positive.

All that changed when we met our new teacher, Barbara Folkenburg, and her husband, Stanley, our new pastor. The Folkenburgs stayed only one year before Stanley joined his brother in full-time evangelism in New York. But that one year changed my life.

Mrs. Folkenburg taught everything with enthusiasm. She opened my mind to the joy of learning. World history involved a year-long project of making a timeline. I still have mine, forty-seven years later! She read us stories of Akhenaton and Evangeline. She created integrated thematic units that involved all parts of the curriculum— an educational concept that didn't become popular until many years later.

Our English term paper was part of both history and typing classes. My paper, about the palace of Knossos on Crete, grew into a lifelong love of archaeology. Mrs. Folkenburg's English teaching was fascinating. She had the gift of being able to explain concepts over and over for the benefit of those who didn't "get it"—without boring the whole class. I can still see her with shoes off, white chalk dust on her cheek, making sure we got the point.

The daughter of missionaries in Central America, much of Mrs. Folkenburg's education had been through correspondence and home-schooling. That might explain why she was such a good algebra teacher—much of what she knew was self-taught. When I took my achievement tests at the beginning of the next school year, my scores had gone up from four to six grade levels in every subject.

Years later we lived only a few blocks from the Folkenburgs' retirement home in Spokane, Washington. Mrs. Folkenburg was still working as a Bible worker in the area. Always into some project or another, she began developing a plan for teaching Bible doctrines to children. She came into my seventh- to ninth-grade classroom to share with my students. That was a precious experience for me.

I know my biology students today at Upper Columbia Academy benefit in some way from Mrs. Folkenburg's teaching so many years ago. A teacher's influence cannot be calculated, even "unto the third and fourth generations."

Gayle (Wilson) Haeger writes from Spokane, Washington, and teaches biology at Upper Columbia Academy.

Reality Check

I was born by cesarean section—and (I believe) already stressed out!
Many of the women in my family are strong-headed Germans who
possess powerful choleric temperaments. I inherited the forcefulness
of my choleric ancestors and combined it with my own perfectionist,
melancholy temperament. Unfortunately, this perfectionism was my
greatest weakness throughout elementary school.

For nearly eight years, schoolwork was my life. My constant push
for perfection in schoolwork meant that I had very few friends. I was
frequently either depressed or stressed out (or both) because of minor
imperfections in one thing or another. Most of my teachers liked
me; I was a straight-A student who always put forth 100 percent of
my effort. But my eighth-grade teacher, Mr. Alexis Emmerson, saw
through me. He managed to look past my grade-point average, past
the powerful front I put on, and deep into the heart of a depressed and
lonely little girl.

It may have been during a parent-teacher conference—I'm fuzzy
on the details—but I do remember the anger I felt toward my teacher
when he confronted my mother and me about my destructive behavior.
Basically, he stated the truth: my obsession over perfection was
detrimental to my mental health. But my simple eighth-grade mind
heard: "You're trying too hard; don't do your best anymore; just give up."
I was furious!

Shortly after this confrontation, our elementary school went through its yearly standardized testing—the Iowa Test of Basic Skills. In a defiant state of mind, I decided to prove my teacher wrong. I would take the test, I would give it minimal effort, and I would fail the test. "Ha! Just look at how poorly I can do if I don't try," I told myself. So I went into the test completely relaxed. I didn't care how badly I did. In fact, the worse I did, the better my point would be made. But my little scheme backfired on me when I received the results of my ITBS test. I had scored higher than I had any previous year!

My relationship with my eighth-grade teacher was a rocky one the rest of that year. He understood, even more than I did, what went on in the deepest part of my mind, and it frustrated me. Many days I found myself going home in tears because of his "insensitivity." I remember one time when I was feeling especially depressed and lonely. I was so miserable I felt ill to my stomach. I begged my teacher to let me call my mom and go home sick. Instead of sympathizing with my pain, he simply, once again, stated the truth: I was not sick; I was just upset. And no, I could not go home.

When I look back on the situation and contemplate the issues I had during that time of my life, I realize how important this "reality check" was to the rest of my life. Because of my eighth-grade teacher, I mellowed out significantly. I realize now that he was not really asking me to do less than my best; he was simply trying to help me lessen the stress in my life. Throughout high school, I remained a straight-A student, but it didn't matter quite so much anymore.

I fear to even think about where I would be today had I carried such a strong obsession for perfection into my high school and college years. Fortunately, I do not have to envision my "what-if" life. Mr. Emmerson saw it for me, and he prevented me from experiencing its outcome. I will be forever grateful to him.

Sara (Cramer) Hiner is a 2006 graduating senior at Pacific Union College in Angwin, California, who plans to enter the teaching profession following her graduation.

Second Chances

Carmen Magray

It's a beautiful sunny morning at Green Bay Junior Academy in Wisconsin, a morning that's still hanging onto summer but grasping for the hand of fall. Everything is going well, and I'm happy to be me—a student teacher, full of ideas, methods, and skills. I have my college stamp of approval, and I'm ready to share my knowledge. However, little do I know that on this particular day, I will step out of my teacher role and become a student again. I will be the one receiving the lesson instead of the one sharing the lesson with my students. It will be a lesson in grace and mercy.

The students are running around the parking lot, their heads bobbing up and down like corks in the open ocean, as they try to increase their endurance for the Presidential Physical Fitness Test to be given later in the year. I'm watching them and enjoying the warm sunshine.

But then I see Peter, a wild card in my handful of students. I never know exactly what to expect with Peter. He has the emotional makeup of a clam, soft and tenderhearted on the inside, but covered by a hard protective shell on the outside. As he is doing his laps, I see him pause, bend over, and choose a stone from the crumbling blacktop in a "David vs. Goliath" manner. But Peter's giant to be slain is not a man ranting against God, but rather a pane of glass in the nearby church window. Peter takes his stone, throws it, and hits his mark. The glass shatters, and I stare in disbelief.

Immediately, I take my wayward student by the hand and march him into the principal's office. He is going to get it now. I have him. I have evidence, and I saw it happen. It's an open and shut case. All that is needed now is for just punishment to be given. I tell Peter to sit down and wait in the principal's office while I go to get the principal. Peter sits there, head dutifully down, knowing that he's blown it again and deserves punishment.

When the principal comes in, I know what is going to happen. I have it all mapped out. At least I think I do. He listens to the retelling of Peter's crime, and, then, with a heart full of grace, tells Peter, "It's OK, Peter. We will take care of it; insurance will cover it."

Wow! That's it? No "What were you thinking?" or "You'd better not do that again!" or "We are going to have a talk with your parents!"? Peter and I both do a mental double take when we realize no punishment will be forthcoming. Peter can't believe his ears. When he finds his voice, he asks the question that's on both of our minds. "Aren't I going to be punished? . . . I was bad." The principal's reply comes with a smile, "No, Peter, you can go now."

Peter stayed in our school that year and never again threw another stone at a window. In fact he stayed ten years at our school. And even though he went through some rough times over the years that followed, he never thought about leaving the school where he was introduced to grace and shown forgiveness by a principal who reflected the character of Jesus.

I learned many lessons during my student teaching, but the one that will always stand out for me is that a rule sandwiched between grace and mercy will always be right.

Thank you, Steve Oust, for a lesson I will never forget.

Carmen (Wilde) Magray writes from De Pere, Wisconsin, and teaches grades one to four at Green Bay Adventist Junior Academy.

She Knew I Needed Special Love

LYNNETTE MCDERMOTT

I was the oldest of four girls and in the second grade when my father came down with polio in the epidemic of 1953. It changed all of our lives. Our stay-at-home mom went to work. We girls were placed with friends, neighbors, and relatives for the first few months while our Dad was hospitalized in two separate hospitals that were filled with polio victims in "iron lungs." During that time, I started third grade with Mrs. Carrie Rockwell, who taught grades three through six at the Whittier, California, Seventh-day Adventist elementary school.

Mrs. Rockwell was very patient with me when I complained of stomachaches and often let me lie on the couch. One day, as a surprise, she arranged for a classmate's mother to take me out of school for an afternoon shopping spree. I returned with two new dresses and a pair of shoes. That church member, Mrs. Swift, showed me special kindness, as she and Mrs. Rockwell realized what our family was going through.

Mrs. Rockwell knew how to make learning fun. I used to beg her to let me take my books home so I could continue my studies, since I enjoyed them so much. But she said school was for learning, and home was for playing and helping around the house. What she did do for me, though, was to let me take grades four and five together, which meant a lot to me. Mrs. Rockwell's confidence in my academic abilities—in spite of my freckles, crooked teeth, and disrupted home—made me love her even more.

Mrs. Rockwell was a loving, caring teacher whose birthday—March 4, 1900—I still remember. She probably started her collection of salt and pepper shakers just to make it easier for us to pick out gifts for her. We loved it when she invited us to her house on the school grounds to see her collection for ourselves. It was fun to look for our contributions.

I wish all children could have at least one "Mrs. Rockwell" during their school years. She will never be forgotten by one little girl who was going through a tough time in her life and who was lucky enough to have her as a teacher for three whole years.

*Lynnette (Vander Mei) McDermott writes from
Highland, California, where she works
as chief of the forensics department
at Patton State Hospital.*

Teacher's Pet

When I first saw her, the day she started teaching at Ernest Amos Spring Junior Academy in Hot Springs, Arkansas, I was in the first grade. Little did I know then that she was the teacher I would learn to love and with whom I would have a lifelong friendship.

"Mrs. Ruby Edwards is my name, what's yours?" she asked me as she prepared to add my name to the list of students in her record book.

"Annette," I said timidly. "Ann-ette," she said, putting emphasis on "Ann."

"No, just Annette," I said.

Looking at me expressionlessly, she wrote my name in her book and quickly moved on to the next child.

The day went well. She settled into her routine, and we all adjusted to our new teacher. I knew there was something special about her—the way she conducted her first- through fourth-grade classroom. She spent time with each of her students, always smiling brightly.

I remember her kneeling to pray with folded hands and closed eyes. I can still hear the way she closed her prayers. "We thank You, Lord, for hearing and answering our prayers. Amen."

When she came to my desk for a little one-on-one time, the first thing she said to me was, "Oh my! Annette, you have the biggest dimples when you smile!" I liked her immediately. I didn't like the way she pronounced my name though. I thought she sounded like a southern belle with an exaggerated drawl.

Through the four years I was in her class, I persisted in trying to have her say my name the way I said it. "Well, your name begins with Ann," she would explain. I had to admit she was right.

As time went on, she made me feel special to her, although she made each of her students feel special. One day, when I was in the fourth grade, I spotted her knitting at recess. My curious nature led me to ask her if I could try a stitch or two. She delighted in showing me how. That led to lessons, and before I knew it, I was knitting with proficiency.

On her fiftieth birthday, I felt badly that I hadn't gotten her a present. But I hadn't known about her birthday beforehand; she announced it only that day. Standing wide-eyed beside her desk, she said, "Class, I'm half a hundred today!" Putting it that way, she received quite a few gasps and astonished looks as we contemplated how ancient she now was.

Although strict at times, Mrs. Edwards was fair, and her character was godly. She loved each of her students. One classmate liked to sing a rhyme to me that went something like this: "Annette, Annette, the teacher's pet!" I thought it was simply awful and wanted to slug him a good one! I don't know if "pet" was the right word, but I do think Mrs. Edwards held me in high esteem. The reason for this might have been because I obeyed and respected her. The boy who jealously created the rhyme usually did not.

All too soon, I was entering the fifth grade and wasn't in Mrs. Edwards's room any longer. I missed her, but I could still peek in her room at recess to say, "Hi."

"Hello, Annette. How are you and those dimples of yours?" she would say, which always made them show more as my smile broadened.

The years went by, and I grew up, graduated, and saw Mrs. Edwards only periodically. Now I'm fast approaching "half a hundred" myself. I saw Mrs. Edwards, now Mrs. Ruby Bozeman, not long ago. At first she couldn't recall my name. Time had taken its toll, and I started to feel sad. I smiled, though, to hide any gloom. At that moment there was a joyful recollection. "Oh, Annette, how are you? I'd know those dimples anywhere!"

There it was. I hadn't heard it in years. That exasperating way she had of saying my name, and suddenly it sounded like music. I started thinking, then, how years can go by and change can take place in many ways, and still some things never change. I thank God for those things. And I thank God for Mrs. Edwards. The time in her classroom seems like yesterday to me, and as I think back on it now, being "teacher's pet" wasn't such a bad thing after all.

Annette Asbury writes from
Hot Springs, Arkansas.

Teacher-Inspired Confidence

KATHRYN SANCHEZ

Mrs. Barbara Perez was an English teacher and librarian at Adelphian Academy (Holly, Michigan) during my junior and senior years. It was a difficult time for me, as I was socially awkward and lacked confidence. I got to know Mrs. Perez in class, in the library, and also when she accompanied our class on a trip. She had a ready laugh, and my friends and I enjoyed her.

At the end of my junior year, she asked me to consider being the newspaper editor the following year. I gave her all sorts of reasons why I wasn't the right person for the job, but she finally convinced me to try. I did, and I ended up getting a scholarship for my work on the paper.

During my senior year, our school held a speech contest with an eighty-dollar prize. That was a lot of money in the 1980s, and I really wanted to win. I knew I could write a good speech, but delivering it—that was something else. I spoke very quickly (I still do) and often failed to enunciate my words. Although I often had to repeat myself to be understood, Mrs. Perez believed I could overcome this bad habit and deliver a winning speech.

Mrs. Perez accepted the challenge of getting me "speech ready." I recited my speech over and over to her in the back room of the library. She patiently worked with me, reminding me to speak more slowly and clearly and had me write "SLOW" in huge letters across my notes. She chose specific words that she had me practice saying clearly. I kept resisting her suggestions, because it sounded silly, like I was talking in slow motion. She told me to trust her and do it the way she showed me. I got discouraged, but she never lost faith in me.

I won that speech contest. I can't recall what I did with the prize money, but I'll never forget how Mrs. Perez's belief in me gave me the confidence to stand up and speak in front of my classmates and teachers.

I lost track of Mrs. Perez after my freshman year in college. I still have a picture of her visiting me in my dorm room with all of my friends gathered around and her laughing with us. My hope is that wherever she is, she reads this and knows how much her time, love, and efforts meant to one shy teenager in her English class.

Kathryn (Gordon) Sanchez writes from Eugene,
Oregon, where she is a homemaker, wife,
and mother of two children.

Thank You for Asking

Wendy Ennis

Although many faculty, staff, and administrators greatly enhanced my experience at Shenandoah Valley Academy, Elder Richard Harris and his wife, Liz, helped change the course of my life forever. He was a retired academy Bible teacher, yet continued to be involved in many aspects of academy life.

One Wednesday evening, toward the beginning of my senior year, the girls' dean noticed I was discouraged. Thinking I might enjoy the time away, she gave me permission to go next door to the church to join the prayer meeting. I was so encouraged by the service that every Wednesday I asked permission to attend prayer meeting. The older folks there quickly enveloped me into their lives.

After one Wednesday evening prayer meeting, Elder Harris and his wife invited me to join them in studying the Bible. I agreed, and we met every Friday just before vespers. It was during one of those Friday evening studies that Elder Harris explained God's simple, profound plan of salvation. "For God so loved Wendy that He gave her His life . . ." Then he asked, "Wendy, would you like to invite Jesus to be Savior and Lord of your life?"

Would I? Yes!

The three of us bowed our heads, and I asked Jesus to come into my heart, wash away my sins, and grant me a place with Him in heaven. All heaven rejoiced! Just before graduation, Elder Harris baptized me.

Life moved on. I went to college, and there God led me to an incredible man who became my husband. Elder Harris officiated at our wedding.

Recently, my husband, Randy, was working late, and I was having bedtime worship with our children. We were talking about Moses and why God wouldn't allow him into the Promised Land. Moses had sinned greatly. Yet God still made a way for His friend, Moses, to be in His kingdom. Then, like Elder Harris had done years earlier, I shared with my children the simple, profound salvation plan God had arranged for people like Moses, who are dirty with sin.

My children listened in rapt attention. In the light coming from the hall, I watched little eyes puddle with tears. Then the Holy Spirit spoke to me, "Ask them to invite Jesus into their hearts." In those quiet, sacred moments, while all heaven exploded with excitement, the older four of our six children asked Jesus to forgive their sins and come into their hearts.

Elder and Mrs. Harris, thank you for following the Holy Spirit's prompting that Friday evening many years ago. The influence of that night when I gave my heart to Christ continues to this day and into another generation. The ripple effect of your ministry will be felt throughout eternity.

Wendy Boyd Ennis lives in Chattanooga,
Tennessee, with her husband,
Randy, and six children.

The Spaulding Factor

KENNETH ALBERTSEN

I have now started my fortieth year of teaching, thirty-five of which have been in Seventh-day Adventist schools. I often think what might have been, as I recall that first year in greater Kansas City, Missouri. Almost immediately following our 1966 summer graduation from Union College in Lincoln, Nebraska, my wife and I moved to an apartment near Cedarvale School in Raytown. Ella Jean was to teach fifth and sixth grades, and I was to teach mathematics and English in grades seven to ten.

After the first week of school, we left with family members to attend a wedding in the hills of Kentucky over the Labor Day holiday, and I was determined that those first few days in the classroom would be my first and last. I was at my wits' end with what I saw as hyperactive seventh- and eighth-graders. I could not remember having been taught how to handle disciplinary problems in the classroom, and it just seemed overwhelming. With twelve or thirteen preparations each day and my felt need to work out all the math problems the day before I assigned them to my students, I felt as though I was starting the year already exhausted.

It was entirely because of Principal Earl Spaulding and his wife, Marty, that I did not "throw in the towel." Earl Spaulding truly was a teacher's principal. He never seemed rattled, and as a teacher in his school, I felt the strong backing of a capable teacher/administrator. His daily encouragement that kept me going.

Only a few months into that first school year, I developed a serious sinus infection and inflamed kidneys and was admitted to Baptist Hospital. I missed nearly a month of school. The doctors couldn't decide if I had a brain tumor, encephalitis, meningitis, or something worse. I was visited often and prayed over many times before my healing. It was Earl's strong encouragement and Marty's nursing attitude that got me back on my feet once again. They insisted that we didn't need the stress of taking summer classes and encouraged us to just relax the following summer. They took us camping and traveling. What a blessed time, and what concern they expressed over and over again.

Earl Spaulding was a genuine Christian, a knowledgeable educator, a handy repair person, a creative builder, a lively outdoorsman, and a bundle of energy. He was happy, friendly, and hard-working. He has given me those goals to which I aim each day. Thank God for this dedicated educator.

Kenneth A. Albertsen writes from Scottsdale,
Arizona, where he teaches math and physics
at Glenview Adventist Junior Academy.

The Teacher Who Saved My Life

SANDRA BLACKBURN

I don't remember anything specific that Mrs. Tooley taught me, although I know she taught me everything I needed to know in fourth grade. What I remember about Mrs. Tooley is that she loved me. She gave me hugs when I was sad; she understood when I had a problem; and she was patient with me when I wanted more work to do. And she probably saved my life.

One morning, while I was talking about some assignment with two of the boys in my fourth-grade class, Mrs. Tooley was standing behind us with her back to us, filing some papers. A button came off my shirt, and lacking a better place to put it, I popped it in my mouth. I continued talking to my classmates until, suddenly, the button slipped down my throat, blocking my airway. I tried to say something. I tried to cough, but nothing happened.

A panicked look came across my face as I motioned to the boys that something was in my throat. They thought I was being funny and started laughing. All of a sudden there was a whack on my back, and the button dislodged and flew across the classroom. I could breathe again!

I turned around and faced Mrs. Tooley who was looking at me with a funny expression on her face. "I don't know why I did that," she said. "Something just came over me, and I turned and slapped you on the back."

I retrieved the button and showed her what she had dislodged from my windpipe. We decided that my angel had directed her to hit me on the back, even though at the time she did it she had no idea why, and we thanked God for intervening in what could have been a tragic situation.

I find it interesting that when I thought of my favorite teacher in elementary school, I first thought of how Mrs. Tooley was kind and loving—and only then remembered she had quite possibly saved my life. I decided I wanted to be like her. My students probably won't remember everything I taught them, but they will definitely remember whether or not I loved them.

Sandra (Dickhaut) Blackburn writes from Columbia, Missouri, where she is a school principal, teaching third and fourth grades.

Trust Conquers Fear

GLENN POOLE II

"Do you want to go rock climbing?" It was Don Kanen, Campion Academy boys' dean for the 1984–1985 school year. I hadn't gone home for home leave that weekend of my sophomore year, and his invitation sounded like a great way to beat the absolute boredom of an empty dorm.

I piled in the car with Mr. Kanen and Marvin Denney, the PE teacher. We headed southwest, past the town of Boulder to Eldorado Canyon. I soon found myself standing at the base of a two-pitch route extending over 150 feet above the trail.

Following Mr. Denney's lead, I climbed to a section just below the top of the first pitch. That final section was overhanging rock and required a layback traverse—a type of move I was completely unfamiliar with. With Mr. Kanen's coaching from below, I successfully made it to the ledge, but not without spending way too much energy on fear. The muscles in my arms, legs, and fingers were like jelly. I was shaking like a leaf in the wind. Dreading the next pitch, I sat quietly while Mr. Kanen climbed and joined us on the ledge.

I was new to rock climbing. I loved the mountains, but growing up in Michigan hadn't provided any such opportunities. I didn't know much about the rope. I'd never fallen while climbing and didn't know that rope, belayer, and equipment worked together to make this a safe sport.

The start of the next pitch was straight up for about twenty feet. Again, following Mr. Denney, I made it about halfway up that section and realized my trembling arms and fingers could hold on no longer. Overcome with the fear of falling the whole seventy feet to the canyon floor below, I screamed out in a terrified voice, "Falling!" as my grip failed.

Of course, being top-roped from Mr. Denney, my "fall" amounted to about one foot, as the rope simply went tight and stretched just a little. With embarrassment now added to my fear and fatigue, I hesitatingly put my feet and hands back on the wall as Mr. Denney literally hauled my 120 pounds up over the cliff to where the climbing was easier.

A week later, early on Sunday morning, school was back in session. The dorm was full of guys—lots of whom loved rock climbing. But when I opened my door in response to a knock, I found Mr. Kanen there again asking me, "Want to go climbing with Mr. Denney and me this morning?" He didn't say where we were going, so I just grabbed my stuff and wondered if I could be just a little less afraid this time.

In the car again with Mr. Kanen and Mr. Denney, I noticed right away that we were headed southwest. Soon we were in Boulder. Passing though town, we made the turn onto the road to Eldorado Canyon. The thought occurred to me that I was being framed. We stopped at the same parking lot we'd used the week before, crossed the same bridge over the same creek, and I found myself, once again, staring up at the exact same wall of rock I'd seen the week before. Mr. Kanen said something like, "This is a pretty good one; I thought we'd try it today."

Again, I was second up, following Mr. Denney. I got to the overhanging crack at the top of the first pitch and put in the traversing layback technique I'd learned the week before. But this time, I moved with a new confidence in the rope's ability to hold me if I fell and quickly found myself on the ledge with Mr. Denney. The muscles in my arms, legs and fingers felt great this time.

Mr. Kanen, climbing third, again joined us on the ledge, and I soon watched Mr. Denney disappear up and over the vertical wall of the next pitch that had so terrorized me the last time. I tied into the rope when it was my turn and minutes later successfully topped the wall under my own power.

Neither Mr. Kanen nor Mr. Denney said a word to explain what they'd done, but remembering their actions nearly moves me to tears to this day. These two men used their time and positions of trust as dean and PE teacher to take a scrawny, scared kid through a process of spiritual initiation. God used their invitations and encouragement to communicate to me, "I believe in you. You can overcome your fear. You can learn to trust. You can conquer your failures. You've got what it takes."

Thanks, Don and Marvin. I'll never forget it!

Glenn G. Poole II writes from Elbert, Colorado.
He serves as the senior pastor at Colorado Springs
Central Seventh-day Adventist Church.

Under Her Wing

In the middle of the 1990s, Carole Hoekenga was the head teacher at Brakeworth Junior Academy in Birmingham, Alabama. The school board invited me to teach the new kindergarten class. I was not a certified teacher, but I felt God was calling me to that work and had given me at least some of the talents needed to do His bidding.

Carole encouraged me to step out in faith and accept the challenge. She then proceeded to teach me how to be a classroom teacher. She showed me how to prepare written lesson plans in order to ensure the class was on course to cover the required material. She taught me how to assess and document what happened in my classroom—both academic achievement and students' personal and spiritual growth. She taught me about using the authority given me as a force for good in the lives of my students and their families. She did all this while providing strong spiritual leadership for the entire school.

I had only a few years under her guidance before she left Birmingham to serve as principal of the elementary school at Mt. Pisgah in North Carolina. She finally retired (too young), but the Lord still had need of her gifts and called her back into service—first as a teacher, and then as a mentor to other teachers.

From time to time, one or another of her former students comes by the school here in Birmingham to ask about her. They testify of her love by their loving remembrances of her. By their lives, they testify of her success as a teacher. By their faithfulness to God, they testify of her spiritual ministry.

Carole Hoekenga is a teacher's teacher. I believe the ever-widening influence of her life of service will prove a blessing to countless people she may never even meet. If I have been of service to God as a teacher, it is because Carole Hoekenga took me "under her wing." I have been privileged to be one of her students, repaying my debt to her by daily trying to imitate her example.

"Of every gift that God has bestowed, leading people to unselfish effort, a record is kept in heaven. To trace this in its wide-spreading lines, to meet those who by our efforts have been uplifted and ennobled, to see in their history the outworking of true principles—this will be one of the studies and rewards of the heavenly school" (Ellen G. White, *True Education*, p. 190).

Carolyn (Casey) Petty writes from Jemison, Alabama, where she teaches kindergarten and pre-kindergarten at Hoover Christian School.

The Day Love Fell

KATHY BOLLINGER

It was one of those days that lasted a whole year. A smog alert had kept my thirty first-graders inside, and they buzzed with pent-up energy. I was eager for the day to end. My husband and ten high school students were waiting for me so we could escape the heat of Los Angeles into the beauty of Yosemite National Park. My backpack, loaded with wilderness necessities, begged me to join it for the drive from southern California up into the pristine mountains.

Reality jerked me back into the moment as Jill and Karen, giggling as usual, pointed to my "love" poster. It swung by one corner. My school was new—brand new! Along with all the luxuries of a beautiful new building came slick painted walls on which nothing seemed to stick. I had used every type of adhesive available, yet posters continually fell.

First thing every morning, I had to put the posters back up on the wall. Some were eventually removed, but I continued to cling to my favorite— my "love" poster. It was adorable. Large pink letters spelled the word "LOVE." Intermingled with the letters were little children. It made such a happy statement and epitomized the atmosphere I wanted in my room. So despite the inconvenience of putting it back up each day, I stubbornly kept it! Using double-stick tape, I once again fastened it in place.

With only an hour left in the day, I announced art time. This was one of the children's favorite events of the week, and my first-graders could hardly contain their excitement. A cheer of glee went up as I produced the little "banana boats" that served as brush-wash vessels for painters. They were off and painting! Childish pictures took on the creativity of unbridled minds while I paced back and forth. My mind was on the road, in the mountains, jumping streams, climbing Half Dome, and simmering dehydrated foods far away from where my body stood.

Then a movement caught my eye as little Charlie stood and attempted to carry his group's murky paint bowl to the sink. "Stop, Charlie," I reprimanded. "You know the teacher is the only one allowed to carry messy bowls to the sink!"

"OK." He smiled as he handed me the bowl and went back to painting. I turned to check the clock again and rediscovered that watched time goes slowly. Hearing a commotion on the other side of the room, I scurried to prevent Phillip and Dannette from flipping more paint at each other.

It was then that I heard a little voice proudly squeak, "Teacher, see how carefully I'm carrying it this time?" I whirled around and saw Charlie, once again, carrying a forbidden container of paint-stained water. In that moment he stubbed his toe and ungracefully flopped to the floor. An indescribable liquid mess oozed into each nearby thread and fiber of new carpet.

Not believing that it had happened—especially just after he'd been told not to carry it—I cried out in frustration, "Charlie, you disobeyed me, and now look at this disgusting mess!" The little boy's face fell. Those trusting eyes that only moments before had shone were now downcast and tear-filled as he looked at me from the floor.

It was only a matter of seconds, but it seemed like eons that we stared at each other in shock. If I live to be a hundred, I will never forget that heavy silence or how it was broken. Woody, perky little Woody, began yelling, "Teacher, Teacher! The love fell!" I looked to where he was pointing, and sure enough, that little pink "love" poster lay on the floor, still quivering where it had fallen. Pushed off the wall by what? Harsh words? Hurry? Frustration?

Sixty eyes followed me as I knelt down beside Charlie. Immediately we were showered with paper towels, and the cleanup began! Never before had a carpet been so lovingly scrubbed, and never before had a poster been backed with more masking tape! Those children wanted to make sure that the love would never fall in that classroom again. So did their teacher!

Thinking back on this incident, I am reminded of the love that our heavenly Father has for us. His love is not dependant on something as fragile as tape on a slippery wall, nor does it waver during an impatient moment. God's love is solid and without condition.

Micah 7:18 speaks of such love. It says, "Lord, who is a God like you? You forgive sin. You forgive your people when they do what is wrong. You don't stay angry forever. Instead, you take delight in showing your faithful love to them" (New International Reader's Version). God's unchanging love is just waiting to be claimed, and there is enough for everyone. I challenge you today to become a student of the Master Teacher, whose love will never fall or fail!

Kathy (Hanson) Bollinger writes from Lincoln, Nebraska, where she is an associate professor of education at Union College.